There He Stands

The Story of

Stonewall Jackson

There He Stands

The Story of
Stonewall Jackson

Bruce L. Brager

MORGAN
REYNOLDS
Publishing, Inc.

620 South Elm Street, Suite 223
Greensboro, North Carolina   27406
http://www.morganreynolds.com

Civil War Titles

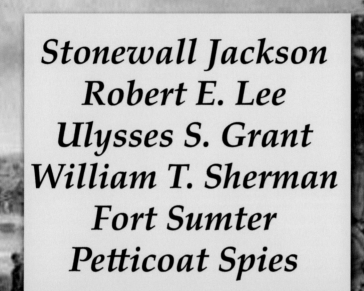

Stonewall Jackson
Robert E. Lee
Ulysses S. Grant
William T. Sherman
Fort Sumter
Petticoat Spies

THERE HE STANDS: THE STORY OF STONEWALL JACKSON

Library of Congress Cataloging-in-Publication Data

Brager, Bruce L., 1949-
    There he stands : the story of Stonewall Jackson / Bruce Brager.—1st ed.
        p. cm. — (Civil War leaders)
    Includes bibliographical references and index.
    ISBN 1-931798-44-3 (lib. bdg.)
    1. Jackson, Stonewall, 1824-1863—Juvenile literature. 2. Generals—
Confederate States of America--Biography--Juvenile literature. 3. Confederate
States of America. Army—Biography—Juvenile literature. 4. United States—
History—Civil War, 1861-1865—Campaigns—Juvenile literature. I. Title. II.
Series.
    E467.1.J15B73 2004
    973.7'3'092--dc22

                                2004014839

Printed in the United States of America
First Edition

Contents

Forging His Path

On the evening of May 1, 1863, in a clearing west of the small northern Virginia town of Fredericksburg, General Robert E. Lee sat with his most famous subordinate, Lieutenant General Thomas J. "Stonewall" Jackson, to make plans for the next day's fight. Their Army of Northern Virginia was pinned down by the Union Army of the Potomac. Lee and Jackson were hard-pressed to see a way out.

That morning, Union general Joseph Hooker had led his forces out of the tangled forest outside Chancellorsville called the Wilderness and attacked Lee from the west. Hooker's attack had been successful, but then he unaccountably pulled back, ordering his men to dig in and establish defensive positions. It seemed he would

Opposite: Thomas J. "Stonewall" Jackson *(Stonewall Jackson House, Lexington, VA)*

wait for Lee to come to him. Lee and Jackson were surprised at Hooker's decision. They planned to attack the next day, even though they were heavily outnumbered.

Then, while Lee and Jackson were discussing their options, Confederate cavalry leader Jeb Stuart arrived with a reconnaissance report on Union positions. The far right of the Union line, he announced, was, in military terms, "in the air"—in other words, not properly defended by or anchored on a natural obstacle. Hooker apparently did not expect to be attacked there. Lee proposed a bold tactic: a wide, flanking movement that would take Hooker's forces by surprise. Jackson was quick to agree.

With their low numbers, making such an attack was a huge gamble. Part of the Army of Northern Virginia was on detached service in the south of the state and unable to take part in the battle. If Jackson took his entire corps on the march, Lee would be left with less than 20,000 men to face the 75,000 men Hooker commanded nearby. Lee and Jackson knew the odds were stacked against them. If they did nothing, Hooker could move to crush their army. If they split their forces to attack from multiple points, they stood at least a chance of success. Before the sun rose the next morning, Jackson was on the road leading his men west.

A legend had already grown up around Stonewall Jackson. His rapid troop movements, lightning-quick attacks, and determination had made him one of the most respected and feared of the Confederate generals. Jackson had come a long way from his humble roots in the hills of western Virginia.

Thomas Jonathan Jackson was born January 21, 1824, in what is now the state of West Virginia. His father's Scotch-Irish ancestors had arrived in America from England in the middle of the eighteenth century, sentenced to terms of service in the colonies as punishment for stealing. They became prosperous in the new world.

Unfortunately, Thomas's father, Jonathan, did not inherit the family's drive to succeed. Several inches shorter than his son's eventual height of just less than six feet tall, Jonathan Jackson was of average intelligence but a bad judge of character. He became a lawyer but was almost always deeply in debt. He also drank too much and gambled heavily.

Jonathan Jackson married Julia Neale, the daughter of a prosperous Irish immigrant merchant named Thomas Neale, on September 28, 1817. Jackson was twenty-seven and she was nineteen. The couple had four children in eight years: two boys and two girls. Thomas Jonathan Jackson, named for his grandfather and his father, was the third child and second son.

When Thomas was two years old, the family experienced a string of tragedies. His older sister died of typhoid, then his father passed away a week later—just one day before the youngest Jackson child, Laura, was born. Jonathan Jackson left his family deeply in debt. Settling these debts required selling the family home.

Julia moved her three surviving children to a one-room house supplied by the local Masonic fraternal order and struggled to make ends meet. Young Thomas had no memories of the father he lost, but Julia Jackson taught her son that his father's irresponsible behavior and lack of self-discipline were to blame for their difficult lives. As an adult, Thomas Jackson would become well known for his strict self-discipline and strong sense of responsibility.

Julia Jackson remarried on November 4, 1830. Her new husband, Blake Woodson, was fifteen years older than his new bride. As Thomas's father had been, Woodson was a struggling lawyer. Seemingly pleasant in public, he was a poor stepfather to Thomas and his two siblings, blaming them for his financial problems. He would, from time to time, suggest to his young stepchildren that they move out.

In 1831, Woodson moved his family 125 miles west to the newly created Fayette County, where he had been appointed clerk of the court. But the family's financial situation did not improve, and between their poverty and Julia's ill health, she soon realized she could not keep her children. Warren, Thomas's older brother, went to live with Julia's family. A few months later, Thomas and Laura were sent to live with an uncle, Cummins Jackson, at a place on the West Fork River called Jackson's Mill. Julia Jackson died a few months later. Thomas was seven years old.

Thomas lived at Jackson's Mill until he was eighteen. It was a beautiful place to call home. Mountain streams

Jackson's childhood home, Jackson's Mill, on the West Fork River in Lewis County, West Virginia. *(Library of Congress)*

form the West Fork River, which flows into the larger Monongahela. This river flows into the even larger Ohio River, which eventually reaches the mighty Mississippi. Jackson's Mill was built on a horseshoe curve in the West Fork, where the river briefly doubles back on itself. Thomas loved the bend. Across the river, there was a narrow flatland just below some foothills. A thick grove of trees there provided shade in the summer. When Thomas needed a break, he would cross the river and rest in the shade of the trees.

A few years after arriving at Jackson's Mill, Thomas and his sister were temporarily removed from Cummins's care. Laura was sent to live with their mother's family, and remained there until she married. Thomas, however, stayed less than a year with another aunt and uncle before he rebelled at their rough treatment and ran away. He returned to Jackson's Mill, where he felt safe. Later, remembering this time, Jackson spoke of the comfort Uncle Cummins provided, saying, "Uncle was like a father to me."

Thomas's life at Jackson's Mill was more financially stable than it had been with his parents, but he missed his mother and father. Cummins did not provide much in the way of parental guidance or discipline. Thomas later wrote his sister that at Jackson's Mill there was "none to give the mandates; none for me to obey but as I chose, supported by my playmates and relatives, all apparently to promote my happiness." When Thomas was twelve, for example, he left for six months with his older brother, Warren, then about sixteen, to seek their fortunes on the Mississippi. Thomas eventually returned to Jackson's Mill, but never spoke of what had occurred during his time away.

At the mill, Thomas was mostly left to fend for himself. He had only a few months of formal education, but somehow developed the determination and initiative that served him so well later in life. He grew into a confident young man, with a personality marked by self-control.

One day in 1842, a few months after he turned eighteen, Jackson found out that his local congressman would be interviewing young men seeking appointment to the United States Military Academy at West Point. (It would be more than a hundred years before women would be admitted.) Jackson went for an interview, eager at the opportunity. Founded in 1802, the academy offered young men the chance to obtain an excellent education in science and engineering in a military setting. Then as now, students had to be nominated by U.S. senators or representatives to be admitted to the academy. Jackson's representative's appointment went to someone else, and the disappointed young man found work as a local constable, mainly collecting debts and serving court papers.

Then news came that the appointee had only lasted one day at West Point. Jackson immediately set about collecting recommendations from as many people as possible. He went to Washington and persuaded his congressman to make him the replacement appointee.

Jackson, in excellent physical condition, had no problem passing the academy's medical examination. By today's standards, the academic portion of the entrance exam was a breeze. The candidate simply had to be able to read clearly, write legibly, and solve a math problem at the blackboard. Jackson, according to witnesses, was sweating as he worked at the blackboard. The next day, the list of those who passed the entrance exam was posted. Jackson's name was at the bottom of the list, but he had passed.

The West Point class of 1846, Jackson's class, was the largest yet. One hundred thirty-three students were appointed by congressmen and senators. Only 123 arrived at West Point in June, 1842, and only ninety-three of these were left by the time the entrance exam was over. Thomas Jackson was one of those young men.

The cadets who passed the entrance exam moved into tents for the two-month summer encampment. The actual academic year began in September, when cadets moved into their barracks. There were two cadets to a room and each cadet had a metal-frame bed, a desk, a chair, and some hooks on which to hang clothing. Little else was allowed in the room. Blankets had to be neatly folded, and when the mattress was not in use, it had to be neatly rolled up on the bed frame. Failure to carry out any of the regulations was one of many ways cadets could earn demerits. If a cadet earned more than two hundred demerits, he would be thrown out of West Point.

This painting from the mid-1800s shows the U.S. Military Academy at West Point, perched on the cliffs of the Hudson River. *(Library of Congress)*

First-year students, called plebes, were constantly harassed by the class above them. Upperclassmen wanted to toughen the cadets, to focus them on the educational experience away from their homes. Harassment was also believed to help develop a sense of community. The plebes were bonded by their misery and quickly learned to turn to each other for moral support. They also got to know each other's strengths and weaknesses.

Jackson, it seems, was the kind of student who made a strong impression. Once, a cadet named Dabney H. Maury was standing outside the barracks, talking with fellow cadets Birkett D. Fry, A. P. Hill, and George Pickett when Jackson came walking up. Maury remarked to the other men, "That fellow looks as if he has come to stay." All four of the cadets watching Jackson would later become generals in the Confederate army.

Jackson made only a few close friends at West Point. Acutely conscious of his poor, rural background, he withdrew into himself, spending little time socializing. He preferred to concentrate on his academic work, which certainly needed his attention. Having had only a few months of formal schooling meant Jackson had to work very hard to catch up. He developed a lifelong desire to improve himself by learning. He learned mostly through reading and, later, by talking with experts.

The tough West Point schedule, rising at 5 AM and having classes and activities scheduled until the lights went out at 10 PM, left very little free time. Jackson's roommates remembered him lying on the floor after lights out, studying by the light of the fire. Some of the few demerits he earned came from being late for morning roll call. Jackson never received a demerit for misconduct during his West Point career.

The West Point schedule called for ten hours of academic work—classes and study time—per day. The educational style of the times focused on rote learning: memorizing and repeating back what the instructor said. Students were kept to a high level of discipline and were expected to obey their instructors without question. Every cadet could be called on to "recite," to solve a problem at a blackboard, every day.

Recitation was a major problem for Jackson. He was very aware of his academic deficiencies and, as a result, became even more uncomfortable speaking in public and solving problems at the blackboard. Jackson would not move on from a problem until it had been solved. Occasionally he had to tell the instructors that he could not solve the day's problem because he still had not solved the problem from the day before. Demerits followed. Professors did not always appreciate Jackson's honesty or his dedication to solving one problem before moving on to the next.

Jackson's first half year at West Point was the most difficult. He barely survived academically. But he would not give up. He vowed that he would "go through or die." After the first year, he began to keep a book of maxims, or proverbial sayings that serve as guides for conduct. "You may be whatever you resolve to be" was one of the first maxims he recorded. He did not invent that idea, but he certainly lived by it. Fundamental to the American national character was the idea that people could improve themselves and their lots in life. Jackson was living this principle.

Seniors, called first classmen at West Point, had the most intensive military education of their four years. They studied a variety of subjects such as geology, constitutional law, and logic. They spent hours on infantry tactics and artillery drill. They also took perhaps the most important course at West Point, the science of war course taught by Dennis Hart Mahan. Cadets studied strategy and tactics, the lessons of the past, and the best ideas of the 1840s on how to win battles. Mahan taught his students that bold, daring generals—but not reckless ones—won battles.

Most of Jackson's fellow cadets never fully warmed to his personality, which could range from shy and reserved to icy—and which never really changed later in life. He was extremely focused, and sometimes his single-mindedness was off-putting. Most cadets failed to realize that Jackson's aloofness was a combination of shyness and a burning desire to concentrate on academic work. Jackson was more interested in accomplishing his goals than in making friends.

His efforts paid off. At the end of his first semester at West Point, Jackson was ranked seventy-first in his class. He would eventually graduate seventeenth out of the remaining fifty-nine members of the class of 1846.

Some of his classmates later said that if the program had lasted a year or two longer, Jackson probably would have graduated first. His hard work was especially remarkable given the highly talented and competitive cadets he graduated with.

Twenty of the fifty-nine members of the class of 1846 would become Civil War generals—some for the North and some for the South. Because these men had studied together at West Point, they knew what their opponents had studied. They also had a good idea of how well those opponents had learned their lessons. The Civil War is remembered for pitting neighbor against neighbor and brother against brother, fracturing friendships and bonds across all boundaries.

While West Point showcased young Jackson's hard work and commitment to his goals, it also helped to define his adult personality. Jackson was drawn to Christianity and spent a lot of time at the academy reading his Bible, but he did not choose a particular denomination for several years. He appreciated the military narratives of the Old Testament and the promises of love and hope—things lacking in his childhood—that the New Testament offered.

During his second year at West Point, Jackson's letters to his sister began to reveal an obsession with his health that bordered on hypochondria. It was hardly unusual for these letters to end with despairing lines, such as: "I am still living, and, with the blessing of God, hope to live for some years to come." Interestingly,

Jackson earned his West Point diploma in 1846. *(Stonewall Jackson House, Lexington)*

Jackson's second year at West Point was also a time when he knew he had passed the hurdle of basic academic survival. He would continue to become more concerned and conscious about his health when his mind was not occupied with academic and military matters.

Jackson's letters expressed the fear that he had consumption and dyspepsia. (Dyspepsia is a catchall term for stomach and digestive problems. The term consumption was commonly used when referring to tuberculosis, the contagious lung disease.) It is highly unlikely that Jackson had tuberculosis because, at the time, the disease was incurable and almost always deadly, and Jackson lived for decades past the time of his worries. But tuberculosis was the disease that had killed his mother, so his concerns were somewhat justified. Likely, Jackson had a bad wintertime cough that was made worse by his imagination.

Upon graduating from West Point, Jackson received the rank of temporary second lieutenant in the United States Army. At the time, army rank and promotion depended on seniority. New West Point graduates, though they would serve on active duty, had to wait for an opening in a regiment until they could gain the full rank of second lieutenant. Jackson's class position at graduation entitled him to assignment in the artillery, second in prestige to the engineers. At the time, artillery consisted of cannon and similar large weapons. Artillery was used primarily to support infantry attacks or to help infantry defend against enemy attacks.

Jackson's first assignment was the Mexican War.

First Taste of Combat

The United States declared war on Mexico on May 13, 1846. Though communication was slow, the students at West Point kept abreast of the trouble along the Mexican border as best they could. That spring, a few months before his graduation, Jackson had written his sister, "rumor appears to indicate a rupture between our government and the Mexican." The rumor was true.

The immediate roots of the war between the United States and Mexico stretched back to 1836, when Texas won its independence from Mexico after a six-month armed conflict. Texas spent the next nine years as an independent nation. Mexico never recognized Texan independence despite the treaty President Antonio López de Santa Anna had signed granting independence. (When he signed the treaty, Santa Anna was a prisoner of the

Antonio López de Santa Anna, Mexican president and army commander.

Texas Army.) After granting independence, Mexico immediately set about trying to take it back. An unstable government was all that kept Mexico from making a full-scale effort to repossess Texas.

The United States recognized Texan independence in 1837, but stayed neutral in the dispute between Texas and Mexico. Americans, however, were strongly sympathetic to Texas and provided some private assistance to the republic. There was always strong support in the South for admitting Texas to the Union. Doing so, however, would upset the balance between slave states and free states in the Senate, since Texas would come in as a state that permitted slavery. The decision over whether or not to grant Texas statehood was complicated by the growing dispute over the slavery issue. Opposition from Northern and antislavery states kept Texas out of the Union until December 1845.

Mexico broke diplomatic relations with the United States over the admission of Texas and sent troops to the Rio Grande, which the United States considered the border between Texas and Mexico. The Mexicans considered the Texas border to be the Nueces River, which flows in a winding course fifty to 150 miles east of the Rio Grande. U.S. president James Polk sent troops, under General Zachary Taylor, to take up positions in the disputed area.

Historians have long debated whether Polk was trying to defend American territory or seeking to provoke a war with Mexico. In truth, his motives were probably a combination of the two. Mexican troops were near the Rio Grande and Polk had to defend what most Americans considered to be national borders. But Polk was also an advocate of what came to be called "manifest destiny,"

This map shows the contested territories of the Mexican War, along with the critical moves and battles of the opposing armies.

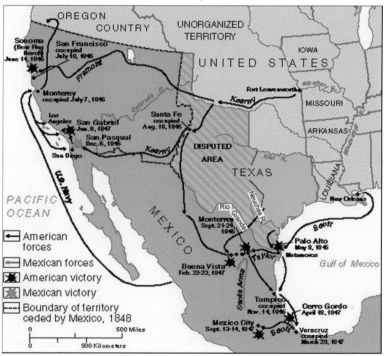

the idea that the natural western edge of the United States was the Pacific Ocean. This included California and the land that is now Arizona and New Mexico, all of which was then Mexican territory. For proslavery Southerners, expansion was attractive because it increased the likelihood that new states would enter the Union as slave states. Opponents of slavery, therefore, opposed the war with Mexico.

Polk and others in his government were pushing the war because they saw an opportunity to take advantage of Mexico's current lack of leadership. They also worried that some other nation—possibly France or Spain—would act first. War between Mexico and the U.S. was all but inevitable.

From the Mexican perspective, General Taylor's soldiers were occupying Mexican territory. On April 13, 1846, the Mexican commander sent a message to Taylor telling him to remove his soldiers. Taylor, backed by President Polk, refused.

A ten-day delay followed until a new Mexican commander took over. On April 23, 1846, two thousand Mexican soldiers were sent across the Rio Grande. They ambushed an American military patrol, killing or capturing all of those soldiers. When word of the incident reached Washington, Congress quickly approved President Polk's request for a declaration of war on Mexico. Because communication was so slow, by the time Congress made its decision, two more battles had occurred on American-claimed soil—at Palo Alto and Resaca de la Palma. Losing the latter battle forced the Mexican forces to withdraw one hundred miles to Monterrey. Taylor and his army followed, seeking to secure American control over southern Texas and remove the threat the Mexican military might pose to this control.

On May 27, 1846, word of the war reached West Point. The graduating cadets, including Jackson, were not particularly concerned with the politics of the issue, but they were eager to see action.

Classes and final exams at West Point ended in mid-June. After graduating, Jackson went to Virginia to visit his family and wait for his orders, which arrived on July 22, 1846. He was assigned to Company K of the First Artillery Regiment. His company commander was Francis Taylor. Though Taylor had twenty years of service, promotions were given so infrequently that he was only a captain. Jackson was told to report to Taylor in New York City. When he arrived, Jackson found that Company K was already on its way to Mexico. Taylor, though, had stayed behind to handle some last minute details and to collect recruits and horses for the company. Taylor, Jackson, thirty recruits, and forty horses finally left New York for Pittsburgh—on foot—on August 19. Fortunately, the rest of their journey would be by boat.

Their party arrived at Port Isabel, Texas, the supply center for Zachary Taylor's army, on September 22. That same day, Mexican troops defending Monterrey surrendered. Travel delays followed, and it was November 24 before Jackson and his fellow soldiers reached

Monterrey. After a few days, Company K joined Taylor's forces in an advance towards Saltillo. To Jackson's disappointment, Saltillo had been abandoned and he did not see action. Jackson also missed the largest battle of the Mexican War, the battle of Buena Vista, which took place on February 22 and 23, 1847. There, Taylor's army eked out victory in a hard-fought battle against the larger Mexican army commanded by Antonio López de Santa Anna.

Santa Anna was an interesting figure—he served as president of Mexico a total of eleven different times. His shifting political alliances brought him in and out of favor. He had been removed from office and exiled to Cuba after conceding Texas to the United States in 1836, but reassumed the presidency in 1846 in order to fight against American forces in the Mexican War.

Not long after the battle of Buena Vista, Taylor arranged an eight-week truce with the Mexican forces. This angered President Polk, who decided to change the high command and focus of the war. Winfield Scott, senior general in the army, was put in command of a second American effort against Mexico. Scott decided to bring an army down the coast of Mexico by sea, landing near Veracruz. This would be the first amphibious invasion in American history. Scott would then march his army 260 miles through hilly terrain toward the capital, Mexico City. Scott assumed this action would force the Mexican government to make peace.

Jackson and his company would join Scott's army.

This depiction of the battle of Buena Vista shows General Taylor leading U.S. forces in fierce combat with the Mexican army. *(Library of Congress)*

Jackson remained anxious to see combat. In early February Jackson met Lieutenant Daniel Harvey Hill, a friend of Captain Taylor. Jackson and Hill went for a walk along the beach, while Jackson eagerly questioned Hill, who had already been in combat. Hill later described the incident in a letter to one of Jackson's aides. According to Hill, Jackson had said, "I really envy you men who have been in action," then smiled and added, "I want to be in one battle."

Jackson's unit took part in the third wave of the American invasion on March 9, 1847. General Scott had only about half the 25,000 soldiers he had hoped to have. But he wanted to get his army out of the Mexican lowlands before the yearly yellow-fever epidemic struck and possibly compromised the troops' health.

On March 22, Scott began shelling Veracruz. The

Mexican forces surrendered five days later. Jackson wrote his sister Laura, explaining how pleased he was with the operation except for one detail: "Allowing the enemy to retire; that I can not approve of in as much as we had them secure and could have taken them prisoner of war unconditionally." Jackson was already showing his desire to win complete victories—to destroy enemy forces, not just force them to retreat.

A few days later, Jackson had the chance to observe and participate in a battle fought more to his way of thinking. Scott's army was using the Mexican National Road to get to Mexico City. It had the advantage of being the best route to advance an army, but the disadvantage was that both sides knew this. A few miles short of the

The Mexican surrender to General Scott at Veracruz. *(Library of Congress)*

town of Xalapa, where the National Road began to rise into the hills, was a narrow pass at a place called Cerro Gordo. Mexican positions controlled the road there and managed to stop the American advance. Scott knew a direct attack was impossible and sent his engineers to find a way around the Mexican position. Captain Robert E. Lee found such a path. Unfortunately, Scott's column of soldiers was spotted and heavily shelled while trying to follow Lee's route around the Mexican position. But they achieved their goal, and a follow-up attack broke the Mexican positions, sending the army fleeing back to Mexico City.

During this battle, Jackson saw firsthand some of the lessons he had learned from Professor Mahan's class at West Point—the value of seeking out the enemy's weak points and the advantage of flanking movements. He also learned the importance of a swift and hard pursuit to keep the enemy off balance. Perhaps most significantly, Jackson also realized his own low tolerance for the cost of war. Seeing a bloated and mangled body on the battlefield, he later wrote, "fill[ed] me with . . . sickening dismay." Jackson knew this squeamishness would have to be overcome, but it made him resolve never to risk unnecessary casualties.

The final lesson Jackson learned was that if an officer wanted to be successful, he had to earn a good reputation in battle. Jackson wanted to win fame, though he recognized how hard it would be to do so. Early on in the war, he wrote his sister: "I presume you think my name ought to appear in the papers, but when you consider the composition of the army, you will entertain a different view; it is such that only those who have independent commands are as a general rule spoken of. . . . If an officer wishes to distinguish himself, he must remain long in the service until he obtains rank; then he receives praise not only for his efforts, but for the efforts of the officers and men under him. That portion of the praise which may be due to me must of course go to those above me, or be included in the praise of the army."

Captain John B. Magruder was the only artillery man to gain real fame from the battle of Cerro Gordo. Magruder and some of his men had been forced to brave enemy fire to join the bulk of their unit. Magruder found some abandoned Mexican cannons, turned them around, and fired a few shots at the retreating enemy. Scott let Magruder's company keep the cannon as a reward for gallantry. Jackson began to consider that a transfer to a unit that seemed to be in the thick of the action might be good for his career. He got himself assigned to Magruder's Company I. Magruder's company was one of four designated to become highly mobile "flying artillery," which Jackson saw as a way to get into the heart of the action. "Flying artillery" was an informal term used at the time for light field artillery that could move quickly around a battlefield. Normal field artillery, though mobile, was too heavy to move quickly. Flying artillery provided close support for infantry, similar to the way air support is used in the modern military.

Jackson, now promoted to a regular commission as second lieutenant, found that Magruder, outside of his dash and bravery in action, was not a popular commander. He was hot-tempered, a severe disciplinarian, and a had a reputation for seeking advancement at any cost—regardless of the risk to his men.

On August 10, Magruder's company moved out, following Scott's advance on Mexico City. By August 16, Scott's army was nine miles from the Mexican capital. There it faced a problem. Mexico City was surrounded on the south and east by two large lakes, swampland, and a virtually impassable lava field. These were excellent natural defenses, and Santa Anna's army made the most of them.

Once again, Scott had Robert E. Lee look for a route around the barriers. Again, Lee found one. It was south of the city and would require improvement to make it passable for troops and artillery. As the Americans set about building a rough road near the small neighboring village of Contreras, the Mexicans shelled their work site. Magruder and another battery were ordered into the area. They were to set up west of the lava field, about a thousand yards from strong Mexican positions, and provide artillery cover. Magruder and his troops did little damage to the Mexican forces but succeeded in distracting their attention from the road's construction and the infantry's advance.

The artillery duel ended on the night of August 19 as darkness fell and a heavy rain came down. Magruder withdrew his guns. Of four, two were damaged and a third destroyed. However, the next day, August 20, Scott was able to attack the Mexican force at Contreras from two directions and push it back. Santa Anna rallied some of his men at the castle of Churubusco and held off the Americans the rest of the day. That night the Mexicans withdrew. Magruder's unit was busy salvaging Mexican cannons and learning how to use them.

Jackson's role in the August 19 artillery duel, including his bravery under fire, earned him a promotion to first lieutenant and a brevet promotion to captain. Brevet rank was given as an honor as well as a temporary rank. At the time, an officer could be assigned to duty at his brevet rank as well as at his permanent rank.

An armistice went into effect soon after the August 20 battle to allow time for peace negotiations. No time limit was set, but both sides agreed to give forty-eight hours notice before ending the armistice. On September 6, with no progress yet made towards peace, Scott terminated the armistice. At dawn on September 8, Magruder's battery, including Jackson, took part in a frontal assault on the fortress at Molino del Rey near Mexico City. The Mexicans were forced out, but at a heavy cost to the attacking Americans. Jackson learned again the dangers of frontal assaults against fortified positions.

Four days later, Jackson took part in the attack on the castle at Chapultepec, the site of the Mexican military college and the last strong point before Mexico City. Magruder's battery was supposed to cover the support-

This striking portrait of Jackson was taken in Mexico in 1847, shortly after he was promoted to first lieutenant. *(VMI Archives, Lexington, VA)*

ing American units, prevent the garrison soldiers from escaping, and prevent Mexican reinforcements from offering help. Magruder and his men were on the extreme left of the American line. The Americans spent the entire first day, September 12, shelling the castle. The actual attack took place early the next morning.

Not long after American infantry began to advance, they ran into heavy fire from a Mexican position alongside the castle. The two infantry regiments that Jackson and Magruder were supporting got stuck. Jackson was sent forward with his two guns into heavy enemy fire.

Every one of the twelve horses pulling his guns and many of his men were killed or wounded. The rest of the men, except for Jackson, took cover. With bullets kicking up directly at him and ricocheting off boulders, Jackson shouted to his men that there was no danger. He would later admit the statement was the only lie he ever knowingly told.

Reportedly, Jackson was standing with his legs spread wide apart when a cannonball flew between them. His bravery inspired an old sergeant to leave cover and help Jackson get one of the guns into position. With great difficulty, they got the gun aimed and began firing back. Jackson later explained why he did not withdraw: "Oh, never, it would have been no disgrace to have died there, but to have failed to gain my point it would."

Soon after they got the gun into place, an American general rode into the area and ordered Jackson and his troops to leave. Deviating from his usual practice of quickly obeying orders, Jackson replied that it would be more dangerous to withdraw than to stay where he was. Magruder rode up, had his horse shot out from under him, and ran to Jackson's side. Magruder and a few of the gunners got the second gun in position, and Jackson began to fire both guns. Jackson's men, seeing the officers exposed to fire but unharmed, came out of cover to join them and help fire the guns.

The general who had ordered Jackson to leave now saw the advantage of staying and ordered a brigade into the area. This brigade carried the outlying Mexican

During the fighting at Chapultepec, Jackson and Magruder were able to turn the tide of the battle. By standing firm rather than retreating, they knocked out an enemy strongpoint that had blocked the American advance. *(Department of Defense)*

position about the same time the Mexican defenses in the castle itself began to collapse.

Santa Anna withdrew and prepared for one final stand at the gates of Mexico City. Jackson found some wagons to which he could attach his guns, thus making them more mobile. His men moved so quickly that they were soon ahead of the main army. There, Jackson ran into Lieutenants D. H. Hill and Barnard E. Bee. He told them he would support them and their fifty men if they wanted to keep going. At this point, Magruder arrived and ordered them to pull back, but he relented when the younger officers begged for permission to keep going.

About half a mile up the road, Jackson's party ran into

1,500 Mexican horse lancers (mounted soldiers whose weapon is a lance), among the best soldiers in the Mexican army. The Mexicans charged, and would have destroyed the Americans had the terrain not forced them to stay on the road in tight formation. Jackson and his two cannons cut a wide swath through the Mexican forces. When they withdrew, Jackson and his men eagerly pursued. Jackson's face would light up when he later described the action. In combat, he had found his element.

Santa Anna withdrew what was left of his forces from Mexico City that night. The next day, September 14, 1847, Scott entered the city. The Americans settled down there for the next six months. Santa Anna resigned the presidency and fled Mexico, leaving the Mexicans without a government stable enough to make peace. The Treaty of Guadalupe Hidalgo was finally signed on February 2, 1848, adding massive new amounts of territory to the United States, including California, New Mexico, Arizona, and portions of several other modern-day states. Unfortunately, gaining this new territory quickly brought the issue of slavery to the forefront of American politics and started the nation on the road to civil war.

Jackson was brevetted major for his actions outside Mexico City. He received a more personal honor a few days after entering Mexico City, at a reception General Scott hosted for all his officers. When Jackson was presented to Scott, the general refused to shake hands. Scott announced, to a now silent hall and an embarrassed

Jackson, "I don't know if I will shake hands with Mr. Jackson!" After a pause, Scott continued, now addressing Jackson, "If you can forgive yourself for the way you slaughtered those poor Mexicans with your guns, I am not sure that I can!" Jackson, never comfortable in crowds, appeared more uncomfortable than ever. Scott then smiled and warmly shook Jackson's hand to applause from the entire room. Scott had a strange sense of humor, but made his point in praising Jackson's conduct in the battles that won the war for the Americans.

Public speaking was not Jackson's strength and never would be, but battle clearly was. The active phase of the war with Mexico had ended, and Jackson could not have guessed how long it would be before he next saw battle.

In late July of 1848, Jackson's artillery company left New Orleans on the long journey to its next assignment—Fort Columbus, Brooklyn, New York. On the way there, Jackson had much time to think about his experiences in the Mexican War. Mexico had reinforced some valuable lessons about how to fight a war. There, Jackson absorbed the lesson of the flanking maneuver—to come around an enemy's side or rear, to hit the enemy were he was weak rather than where he was strong. He observed that the bold commander would triumph over the cautious commander. Jackson also learned that the army had to be properly supported with supplies and medical care for it to function effectively. He saw how filthy a military camp, including its hospitals, could be. At the time, the link between poor sanitation and disease was not widely known, but disease and infection actually killed more soldiers than did enemy fire. Jackson sensed that filthy conditions were bad for discipline, bad for morale, and bad for military effectiveness.

During the war, Jackson learned some additional things about military life that were possibly even more important to him than battle strategy. He learned that war was his natural element, a situation in which he could, and did, excel. For Jackson, a career in the military was the perfect career. The military gave Jackson the sense of order and discipline he had lacked in his childhood and seemed to thrive in as an adult. The military also appealed to Jackson's sense of duty. He saw battle as an invigorating opportunity for advancement, a place away from ordinary concerns where his life could gain focus.

Peacetime Soldier and Teacher

In the middle of the nineteenth century, Brooklyn, New York, was an independent city. It did not become part of New York City until 1898. Once there, Jackson and his comrades had little to occupy themselves with besides the ordinary duties of a peacetime encampment.

With no military action pending, Jackson again became obsessively concerned with his health, and he addressed his health concerns with the same determination he applied to all his other endeavors. He read, studied, and talked with people to find methods for alleviating his various aches and pains—including a weak stomach and rheumatism. Jackson came up with some unusual practices, such as not eating pepper on the grounds that it would make his left leg heavier than his right. Even if it had no effect on leg weight, giving up pepper would have been a good idea for someone with stomach trouble. Jackson adopted the principle of giving up food he liked too much. He stringently followed a plain, unseasoned diet—even bringing his own food when he accepted a dinner invitation. His one indulgence was his overwhelming fondness for fruit.

Jackson's rheumatism, which may well have been the early onset of arthritis, was likely alleviated somewhat by the "water cure"—sitting in hot baths—that he liked. The doctor who convinced him to socialize more and exercise regularly certainly hit on a way to help improve Jackson's general condition and mood.

When he returned from Mexico, Jackson was concerned about more than just his physical health. He had begun feeling the need for formal religious affiliation to match his growing religious faith. In Mexico, Jackson had met with the Catholic archbishop there, as part of his investigation of that faith. But Catholicism is a highly organized religion very dependent on ceremony, and Jackson wanted something simpler.

The first church Jackson seriously considered joining was the Episcopal Church. His friend and commanding officer upon returning from Mexico, Captain Francis Taylor, was Episcopalian. The man who had been the West Point chaplain while Jackson was a student was also Episcopalian. Jackson was eventually baptized in April 1849 as a member of the Episcopal Church. He began attending services regularly. But the Episcopal service, like the Catholic, is very formal, and Jackson kept looking for a faith in which he felt more comfortable.

On October 1, 1850, Jackson was transferred to Company E of the First Artillery. Captain William H. French, like Jackson a brevet major, was the commander. Jackson had known French for three years, but they were no more than acquaintances. The company was being transferred to Fort Meade in central Florida to keep order there in the aftermath of the Seminole War. (The conflict between the United States and the Seminole—Native Americans who inhabited Florida—began in 1835 and was the most costly of all the Indian wars.)

The transfer to a warm climate was initially a welcome change from the cold winter of New York harbor. Then Jackson and French began to clash. French shared some personality traits with Jackson, including a concern for advancing his military career and being a stickler for discipline and duty. Neither of the men struck others as being particularly friendly. But Jackson tended to be polite and courteous, while French leaned toward being abrasive.

The first sign of trouble came when French started sending out patrols to find any remaining Seminole in Florida. After signing treaties with the U.S. government when the war finally drew to an end in 1842, the Seminole had been sent to Oklahoma, then called Indian Territory. But about three hundred remained in Florida, and though most of them wanted to live in peace, a few would occasionally raid white farms, primarily for the sake of survival. Jackson was sent out with a scouting

Captain William H. French. *(Library of Congress)*

party in late January 1851, and then again a month later, to explore the area and locate any remaining Seminole. Both expeditions took about a week. Not surprisingly, considering there were very few Seminole spread out over a large area, Jackson's men did not find any.

Jackson was somewhat disappointed. He wrote his sister on March 1, 1851, "I like scouting very much, as it gives me a relish for everything; but it would be more desirable if I could have an occasional encounter with Indian parties."

When Jackson had nothing to report back to French, French claimed Jackson had failed to carry out his orders. French decided he would lead the next expedition himself. Most of his men, including Jackson, interpreted this as a lack of confidence in their ability. This caused tension in their ranks.

Around the same time, Jackson received a letter from the superintendent of the Virginia Military Institute (VMI), asking if he would be interested in being hired as a professor of Natural and Experimental Philosophy. This is the field we generally call physics today, but it included other sciences as well. Jackson's name was apparently given to the superintendent of VMI by D. H. Hill, whom Jackson had met in Mexico. A Virginia state senator who was a distant cousin also recommended Jackson. Before going to West Point, Jackson had a brief experience teaching to a small class at a one-room schoolhouse. There is no indication he either enjoyed it or was very good at it, and it is unclear whether VMI even knew about this background.

Because the United States was now at peace, many promising young officers were leaving the military because they saw little chance for advancement. Jackson was not overly excited about the idea of teaching at VMI. However, the job was in his home state and was, at least, still in a military environment. If another war began, he thought, being a respected teacher at VMI might help his chances of earning a high-ranking position in that war. Jackson replied right away, accepting the superintendent's offer to place his name under consideration.

Meanwhile, Jackson's relationship with French continued to sour. After being denied a transfer to another company, Jackson applied for a nine-month leave of absence with permission to leave the country. He was thinking about visiting Europe. But events in March gave him pause.

French decided to move Fort Meade, their post, to a better location in the area. Jackson was put in charge of construction of the new post. Jackson's increased authority rankled French, who chastised his subordinate for being too independent. Jackson did not comment directly on the situation, but it seems he did not respond well to French's criticism. Their already-testy relationship was probably made worse because both held the brevet rank of major. Jackson might have felt that French did not actually outrank him.

When French requested that higher-ups evaluate the situation, it was determined that French was in charge and Jackson under his command. Jackson was criticized for behaving discourteously to a senior officer. He was outraged when he realized that French had been making personal and professional complaints about him.

Someone leaked word to Jackson that French might be having an affair with a young servant girl living in his household. French was married, and his wife was at the post. Jackson decided to investigate the affair and started questioning the enlisted men. The men had no intention of being caught in a feud between officers. They reported the questioning to the first sergeant, who went directly to French. French had Jackson placed under arrest and confined to the fort. The day he was arrested, Sunday, April 13, 1851, Jackson broke his personal rule against writing letters on the Sabbath and wrote to headquarters, asking to be released from arrest and allowed to pursue his investigation.

The next day, Jackson filed formal charges against French for conduct unbecoming an officer, referring to his alleged affair. Two days later, French returned the favor, accusing Jackson of attempting to injure the private reputation of an officer. French also arrested Second Lieutenant Absalom Baird, whom he accused of conspiring with Jackson. By the end of April, all of these charges had been rejected by the military. A few days later, Jackson accepted the formal offer of a professorship at VMI. He was put on official leave, pending his departure from the company.

It was probably lucky for Jackson that he got out when he did. Though nothing came of the charges, French still refused to drop them, even after Jackson left the post. Jackson might have showed poor judgement by investigating his superior officer's private life, but French was clearly a difficult man to get along with. Within a year's time he had filed charges against every officer under his command, including the officer who replaced Jackson.

But in May of 1851, Jackson was on his way to new

The fortress-like Virginia Military Institute, where Jackson taught for ten years. *(VMI Museum, Lexington, VA)*

adventures: a teaching career at the Virginia Military Institute. VMI was founded in 1839 to serve as a military college, a function it continues today. Unfortunately for his students, Jackson based his teaching method perhaps a little too closely on the style used at West Point. Jackson was not an expert at physics. He would learn his material the night before a class, memorizing pages from a book. The next day, he would recite the material in front of his class. If the students understood, fine. If a student asked a question, though, Jackson would simply back up and recite the misunderstood part over again. He considered any further questions to be acts of insubordination.

One incident that occurred in May 1852, at the end of Jackson's first year at VMI, reflects his teaching style. He sent Cadet James A. Walker to the blackboard, as Jackson later explained, to find the "hour angle of the sun. His result was not obtained in a manner satisfactory to me. I sent him to his seat, he asked me in what his error consisted. I considered his manner disrespectful." Jackson did not explain what he meant by "disrespectful," and when Walker pressed the matter, Jackson "told him that all I required of him was that he should behave himself." The next time Walker was asked to recite at the blackboard, further confrontation ensued, and the student was eventually brought to a court martial.

At his trial, Walker said that he had simply been misunderstood and that Jackson was not good at dealing with people. He complained of Jackson's "singular and eccentric notions" and "rigidity of adherence to the letter of his instructions." The court martial board agreed with Jackson, however, and Walker was expelled for serious insubordination. Walker was so upset he later challenged Jackson to a duel. Jackson ignored the challenge, but Walker was considered sufficiently dangerous that his father was asked to come to VMI to take the young man home. Interestingly, Walker later served under Jackson during the Civil War. There is no indication that they had any problems getting along then.

Though VMI ruled in Jackson's favor, the evidence

suggests that he was not a very good teacher. His students later remembered that Jackson could sometimes be persuaded to answer questions about his experiences in the Mexican War. During those times they found him far more relaxed and approachable.

A few important things came about during Jackson's ten years at VMI. Soon after arriving in Lexington, he renewed a friendship with D. H. Hill, whom he had met in Mexico. Hill had also left the army and was teaching mathematics at Washington College. At Hill's suggestion, Jackson began to investigate the Presbyterian Church. Jackson liked the church's doctrines, particularly the idea that the individual controlled his or her own salvation. He also liked the simplicity of the religion and joined the church in December 1851. He eventually became a deacon and remained close to the church for the rest of his life.

About a year later, Jackson began courting Elinor Junkin, daughter of the president of

Jackson's first wife, Elinor Junkin. *(VMI Archives, Lexington)*

Washington College. They were married in August 1852. Because of a shortage of housing in Lexington, the couple lived in a wing of the Junkin house. In October 1854, Elinor Jackson died while giving birth to a still-born son. Jackson was crushed. He tried to avoid public demonstrations of his grief, but people noticed how drained he looked. Jackson sought to fight his grief by throwing himself more fully into his religion, trying to find some divine reason for the deaths of his wife and son.

Around this time, Jackson and respected VMI professor John Preston started a Sunday school for African Americans. Jackson was a strict but popular teacher, and sometimes his classes would have as many as eighty or a hundred students. Jackson would read passages from the Bible and offer his interpretation, and then the class would break into smaller groups to study the Bible more closely. Possibly some of the students learned to read by this process, in violation of the Virginia law that forbade teaching slaves to read or write for any reason. There is no indication that Jackson ever bothered to respond when some Lexington citizens raised the issue that slaves might be learning to read in Jackson's class. Jackson's school gradually gained acceptance in Lexington, and Jackson himself contributed financially to the school for the rest of his life.

During his tenure at VMI, Jackson met and married his second wife, Mary Anna Morrison, a sister of D. H. Hill's wife. Their first child, born on April 30, 1858, would die within a month. The grief caused by this

Jackson's second wife, Mary Anna Morrison. *(VMI Archives, Lexington)*

child's death was horrible for them both. Anna was subsequently ill for many years, and Jackson showed that even though he was a tough military commander, he was also a loving, solicitous husband.

The couple was separated for much of their marriage; Anna was often sent away for treatment and then Jackson went to war. Through it all, they managed to keep up a steady correspondence. Their home in Lexington had a beautiful garden that Jackson was devoted to. In his typical fashion, he set out to learn all he could about gardening. Jackson's letters to Anna when she was away were full of news about the garden. Most of all, he wished for her to regain her health: "My little pet, your husband was made very happy at receiving two letters from you and learning that you were improving so rapidly. I have more than once bowed down on my knees, and thanked our kind and merciful Heavenly Father for the prospect of restoring you to health again." Anna eventually bore a second child, Julia, in November of 1862.

Jackson's household included six slaves. Little direct evidence exists about Jackson's attitude toward slavery. He neither endorsed nor spoke against the institution. The little we know about Jackson's views come to us through his second wife, Anna:

> It has been said that General Jackson 'fought for slavery and the Southern Confederacy with the unshaken conviction that both were to endure.' This statement is true with regard to the latter, but I am very confident that he would never have fought for the sole object of perpetuating slavery. It was for her *constitutional rights* that the South resisted the North, and slavery was only comprehended among these rights. He found the institution a . . . responsible and troublesome one, and I have heard him say that he would prefer to see the Negroes free, but he believed the Bible taught that slavery was sanctioned by the Creator himself. . . . He therefore accepted slavery, not as a thing desirable in itself, but as allowed by Providence for ends which it was not his business to determine.

Cotton plantations, worked by slaves, were the foundation of much of the Southern economy before the Civil War. *(Museum of Fine Arts, Boston)*

Near the end of 1859, a South Carolina planter worried about increasing agitation over slavery wrote, "We are looking to some sudden turn of fortune we know not what to rescue us from the doom we have not the courage to avert." The question of slavery would eventually split the country in two.

At the start, slavery was an economic measure, first implemented in Virginia in 1619—ten years after the establishment of Jamestown, the first successful English settlement in America. Africans were captured or purchased in their native countries and brought to the colonies to serve as the labor force for the growing economy. The economic system of this new world was soon totally dependant on slave labor.

When the United States declared its independence in 1776, all thirteen states allowed slavery, though slavery was far more common in the Southern states. By the early 1800s, Northern states had banned slavery. Slavery also seemed to be dying out in the South. Then, in 1793, a man named Eli Whitney invented a device called the cotton gin. The gin made it far easier to process cotton, which greatly increased the demand for that crop. Picking cotton is extremely labor intensive, and in the South that labor came from slaves.

As the Southern states continued to develop an agrarian economy—made possible by the existence of slavery—the North was expanding its manufacturing infrastructure. This divergence, combined with important geographical differences between the South and the North, helped create a wedge that soon separated the two regions' economic and political interests. The debate over slavery came to epitomize that divide. Several efforts were made to try to settle the issue. In 1820, the Missouri Compromise admitted the state of Missouri to the Union as a slave state and the state of Maine as a free state, where slavery was not permitted. The compromise maintained a balance between the number of free states and the number of slave states. It also drew a line from the southern border of Missouri. All new states above the line, except for Missouri, would be free; below the line would be slave.

Former president Thomas Jefferson saw dangers in the compromise. Jefferson, writing to a friend in 1820, described the American split as "a firebell in the night," silenced only "for the moment" by the compromise, which "awakened me and filled me with terror." Jefferson saw what a later writer in another circumstance called a "fault line" between the North and the South, a "geographic line, coinciding with a marked principle, moral and political, once conceived and held up to the angry passions of men, [which] will never be obliterated; and every new irritation will mark it deeper and deeper."

Adding enormous amounts of new territory with the end of the Mexican War, which Jackson had helped win, effectively destroyed the Missouri Compromise. The South had no intention of allowing the Mexican prohibition on slavery to remain in effect, which would have allowed the new territories to become free states. Southerners saw the new territories as ideal for the expansion of slavery that they felt was needed if their slave-dependent economy were to survive. Some Southerners began to demand that the U.S. government guarantee that slavery would be allowed to continue.

The final effective compromise on slavery came in 1850. However, this Armistice of 1850 only lasted four years. In 1854, Senator Stephen A. Douglas of Illinois introduced a measure to formally organize the Nebraska Territory. It would be divided into two territories, which eventually became the states of Kansas and Nebraska. Douglas introduced the concept of popular sovereignty in this legislation. According to this principle, the people of each state or territory could decide for themselves whether they would allow slavery. This seemed in keeping with the basic American principle of local self-government. It also was an invitation to trouble in Kansas.

Southerners refused to accept that slavery could be banned in the territories, even if the people there wished to do so. Increasingly, Northerners wanted to stop the spread of slavery. Kansas became their battleground and so-called "bleeding" Kansas—a violent

Senator Stephen A. Douglas. *(Library of Congress)*

clash between pro and antislavery factions—followed. The crisis came to a head when the Lecompton Constitution of 1857, named after the small town in which it was written, authorized slavery in Kansas. This constitution was immediately challenged, its opponents arguing it had been approved in an unfair referendum.

U.S. president James Buchanan and Southern representatives urged Congress to accept the results of the vote and grant Kansas's statehood. Senator Stephen Douglas broke from the normally proslavery mainstream of the Democratic Party and led the successful effort to reject the Lecompton Constitution. Douglas felt the procedures followed in Kansas were a gross violation of

This map shows the breakdown of states that supported slavery (the South) and free states (the North) in 1861. Oregon and California were supporters of the North, but were too far away to contribute militarily.

what he had meant by popular sovereignty. One year later, when a fair vote was finally held in Kansas, the Lecompton Constitution was overwhelmingly rejected. Kansas would be admitted to the Union as a free state in 1861.

At the end of 1857, even before the final votes, a Kentucky editor summarized the effects of Southern support for the Lecompton Constitution: "The South never made a worse move. . . . both a blunder and a crime . . . it is calculated to break down the only national party in one section of the Union. A contest for president will be purely sectional, and we know how this will end; and then the object of the disunionists will be near its accomplishment."

Stonewall

Jackson had not previously taken much of an active interest in politics. Jackson's wife, Anna, later wrote, "At this time [1860] Major Jackson was strongly for the Union, but at the same time he was a firm State's-rights [sic] man. [Advocates of states' rights favored state over federal power in most domestic matters.] In politics he had always been a Democrat, but he was never a very strong partisan." Jackson was well traveled and well educated, far more so than many Americans of the time. However, his personal loyalties were towards his locality and state, quite typical of Southerners at the time.

Jackson's lack of political involvement began to change in 1859. In late October, word reached Lexington of John Brown's raid a few days before on Harpers Ferry, Virginia (now in West Virginia), about one hun-

John Brown and the insurgents set up fort in an engine house in Harpers Ferry.
(Library of Congress)

dred miles north of Jackson's home in Lexington. Brown had hoped to arouse the biggest fear of Southerners, a violent slave rebellion. Militarily, the raid was a failure. Brown and his men attacked the federal arsenal, took a few hostages, and held them for a day until U.S. troops under Colonel Robert E. Lee—the same scout Jackson had served with in Mexico—captured Brown and his surviving men and freed the hostages. On November 2, 1859, Brown's trial by Virginia authorities ended in a death sentence.

The incident at Harpers Ferry had the effect of raising the stakes in the dispute between the North and the South and probably made the Civil War inevitable. John C. Tidball, a friend of Jackson's, later wrote of the raid: "Although the enterprise failed so signally, it carried consternation through the South and deep excitement in the North. More than any other event which had up to this time happened, this intensified the bad feeling then existing between the two sections."

Jackson led one of two contingents of VMI cadets sent to keep order at Brown's execution. He wrote his wife twice from Charlestown, the site of Brown's hanging. Initially, he reported, "There are about 1,000 troops here, and everything is quiet so far. We don't expect any trouble. The excitement is confined to more distant points."

John Brown, leader of the rebellion at Harpers Ferry. *(National Portrait Gallery, Washington, D.C.)*

The evening of the execution, Jackson again wrote his wife: "John Brown was hung today at about $11^{1/2}$ AM . . . He behaved with unflinching firmness. . . . I was much impressed with the thought that before me stood a man, in the full vigor of health, who must in a few moments be in eternity. I sent up a petition [a prayer] that he might be saved."

During the summer of 1860, Jackson and his wife went to Northampton, Massachusetts, for hydrotherapy at a popular spa called the Round Hill Water Cure. There, the Jacksons sensed the growing feelings of tension and hostility among some of the Northern guests. As Anna later wrote, while at the spa Jackson "heard and saw enough to awaken his fears that it might portend civil war; but he had no dispute with those who differed from him, treating all politely and [making] some pleasant acquaintances."

Back in Lexington, the community was divided between pro-Union residents, including Jackson, and those—including many of the students and faculty of VMI—who advocated secession. Jackson's position was simple: he hoped the Union would endure; he hoped to see everything possible done to keep the peace, but if all else failed he would be prepared to fight. He tried to maintain his belief that God would find some solution to the crisis that seemed to be dividing the nation.

That same year, the Democratic Party nominated Stephen Douglas for president. Many Southerners left the party in protest—they had not forgotten Douglas's opposition to the Lecompton Constitution, his work for the Kansas-Nebraska Act, or his support of popular sovereignty. Southern Democrats opted to nominate their own candidate, John C. Breckinridge. This party split marked the beginning of the end—the country's divides were now too deep to mend. After the Democratic Party split, a strongly secessionist newspaper, the *Charleston Mercury,* declared, "The last party, pretending to be a national party, is broken up and the antagonism of the two sections of the Union has nothing to arrest its fierce conclusions."

Abraham Lincoln, a member of the newly formed and antislavery Republican party, was elected president of the United States in November 1860, in a four-man race. Southerners did not believe Lincoln's assurances that he would not interfere with the continuation of slavery where it already existed. Lincoln, they felt, would at the very least oppose slavery's expansion, and if slavery could not expand, many influential Southerners felt it would die out.

One month later, South Carolina voted to secede from the Union. Florida, Georgia, Louisiana, Mississippi, and Alabama left within the next two months, and Texas seceded in March, making it official about an hour before Abraham Lincoln took the oath of office as U.S. president. After seceding, these Southern states established themselves as the Confederate States of America (the Confederacy), with an independent government separate from that of the United States.

ABRAHAM LINCOLN,
SIXTEENTH PRESIDENT OF THE UNITED STATES.

The newly elected president, Abraham Lincoln. *(Library of Congress)*

In January 1861, two months after Abraham Lincoln was elected president, Jackson wrote to his nephew expressing his view of the political situation: "I am in favor of making a thorough trial for peace, and if we fail in this and the state is invaded to defend it with terrific resistance. . . . I desire to see the state use every influence she may possess in order to procure an honorable adjust[ment] of our troubles; but if after having done so, the free states instead of permitting us to enjoy the rights guaranteed to us, by the Constitution of our Country, should endeavor to subjugate us, and thus excite our slaves to servile rebellion . . . it becomes us to wage such a war as will bring hostilities to a speedy close."

Jackson went on to say that he did not expect Virginia to leave the Union. He thought that once Virginia proved to the North its willingness to secede, the North would give in and protect the existence of slavery. A month later, he expressed the same thoughts to his sister, but added, "after we have done all that we can do for an honorable preservation of the Union, there shall be a determination on the part of the Free States to deprive us of our right which the fair interpretation of the Constitution, as already decided by the Federal Courts, guarantees to us, I am in favor of secession."

The question of whether or not Virginia would secede was settled by a drastic event that took place in South Carolina. At 4:30 on the morning of April 12, 1861, Confederate forces opened fire on Fort Sumter, the fort run by U.S. troops that guarded the entrance to the harbor of Charleston, South Carolina. Lincoln had refused to remove Federal troops from their post after South Carolina seceded from the Union. After a thirty-six-hour bombardment, the Federal troops surrendered.

Lincoln responded by calling for volunteers to help settle the crisis. Arkansas, North Carolina, Tennessee, and Virginia responded to Lincoln's call by seceding.

This portrait of Jackson was taken during his tenure as an instructor at VMI. *(VMI Archives, Lexington)*

The four remaining slave states—Maryland, Kentucky, Missouri, and Delaware—would stay in the Union.

On the evening of April 12, before word reached Lexington that fighting had started at Fort Sumter, Jackson was asked to speak at a meeting of VMI cadets and staff. Rumors of pending war had long been in the air, and now Jackson addressed them. His statement was brief: "Military men make short speeches, and as for myself I am no hand at speaking anyhow. The time for war has not yet come, but it will come, and that soon, and when it does come, my advice is to draw the sword and throw away the scabbard."

Five days later, the Virginia secession convention voted to leave the Union. Four days after that, Jackson led the VMI cadets to Richmond, where they helped train and organize the many volunteers coming in from around the state. On April 26, Jackson became a colonel in the Virginia state forces. Three days later he was assigned to his first command, Harpers Ferry.

Harpers Ferry is located northwest of Washington, D.C. in what is now West Virginia, where the Shenandoah River flows into the Potomac. It was the arsenal there, one of the largest producers of rifles and pistols in the United States, that had been the immediate target of John Brown's raid. The small town of Harpers Ferry sat at the entrance to the fertile Shenandoah Valley, which would produce much of the grain used to feed the eastern Confederate armies. Harpers Ferry was an important strategic location because it controlled the main east-west railroad, road, and canal. Virginia state troops had captured Harpers Ferry on April 19, a move planned even before Virginia seceded.

The first problem Jackson faced on arrival at his new command was what to do about the mass of untrained volunteers he found there. Jackson's second problem would be defending Harpers Ferry. The town, and what was left of the armory, sits in a small valley surrounded on three sides by hills. The greatest problem was Maryland Heights, across the Potomac. Artillery pieces mounted there could destroy Harpers Ferry. Maryland, though a slave state, was still part of the Union. The political situation was touchy; Jackson could not simply send troops across the Potomac to seize the heights.

Jackson began training the troops at Harpers Ferry

Although undersized and homely, Little Sorrel was the favorite mount of Jackson, who appreciated the horse's intelligence and toughness. Little Sorrel was beloved throughout the Confederacy. Southern ladies would clip hairs from his mane and tail to make wristlets and rings. *(VMI Archives, Lexington)*

just after his arrival. He soon gained a reputation as a hard taskmaster, one who seemed to be everywhere at once but who was also fair. The soldiers knew that their commander subsisted on the same rations and amount of sleep as they did, if not less. He made a point of dressing in a simple, even shabby, manner. In keeping with Jackson's belief that patience, modesty, and diligence made good soldiers, he led his men by example. He did not berate them for mistakes, only for lack of effort. Troops soon came to gladden at the sight of their commander on his legendarily tough horse, Little Sorrel, as the two made their rounds.

While Jackson was at Harpers Ferry, he suffered a loss of a more personal kind. His only surviving sister,

Laura Arnold, was extremely vocal in her support of the Union. Once, the two had been very close; Jackson wrote to her regularly for years. But when the war came, each chose a side and, as far as is known, they never spoke again. Jackson's last letter to her, written just a week before the attack on Fort

Jackson's sister Laura Arnold. *(VMI Archives, Lexington)*

Sumter, betrays the grief he felt at their falling-out, and states how much he wished she would reconsider her views on God (she was an agnostic) and the pending war: "When a cloud comes between you and the sun, do you fear that the sun will never appear again?" Jackson's faith was strong, and he wished his sister could share it.

Brigadier General Joseph Johnston arrived to take command of Harpers Ferry on May 25, 1861, three days after Virginia voters approved secession and joined the Confederacy. Johnston was impressed with what Jackson had done to organize the troops in the area. When Johnston formally organized the men into brigades,

Jackson was given command of the First Brigade. Johnston also realized that Harpers Ferry could not be defended. In mid-June he withdrew his forces about twenty miles southwest to a better position. The armory equipment that could not be moved was destroyed.

Pierre Gustave Toutant Beauregard, who had been in charge of the firing on Fort Sumter in Charleston, now commanded a larger Confederate army in the area of Manassas, Virginia, about twenty-five miles west of Washington. The main Federal army, under Irvin McDowell, was at Washington. A second Federal army, under Robert Patterson, was in Maryland, not far from Johnston's position near Harpers Ferry. Most commanders guessed that the main Federal effort would be a move by McDowell against Beauregard. The Northern press, political leadership, and general public had taken up the cry of "On To Richmond!" (Richmond was by this point the capital of the Confederacy), and McDowell was being pressured to

Union general Irvin McDowell. *(Library of Congress)*

Federal cavalrymen fording Bull Run. *(Fondation Saint-Louis, Amboise, France)*

take action before he felt his forces were ready. Patterson was given the task of keeping Johnston's army from supplying Beauregard's with reinforcements.

On July 16, 1861, McDowell's force began its advance from Washington, D. C. to Manassas. Beauregard notified Johnston, who began to make arrangements to move his army to intercept. Both sides moved slowly. Not only were the Union commanders tentative about moving their troops into the South, but an army could move no faster than its soldiers could walk, and it certainly could not outpace its support wagons. While men could make twenty or thirty miles in a day, heavy wagons laden with supplies and food were not so easy to maneuver. Where roads were scarce or terrain especially difficult, progress was slowed even further.

Jackson, now a brigadier general, got his orders to move to Manassas early on the morning of July 19, 1861. His men began to march eastward, through Winchester. At one point, several Winchester businessmen stopped Jackson. They were unhappy to see Confederate troops leaving the area. One asked him, "General Jackson, are you going to take these Virginia boys away from here, and leave us to the horde of Yankees who are coming down upon us? Let the other people go and you stay here!" Jackson, according to an aide, responded only, "I am a soldier and obey orders." The aide noted that, despite his abrupt tone, Jackson's "face was more full of mental anguish and grief than I had ever seen it before."

By midafternoon, after a leisurely march, Jackson's men had cleared Winchester. There he finally let them know where they were headed. The next morning, they had reached the railroad where they boarded trains for the thirty-five-mile ride to Manassas. The men would later remember this march as one of the most relaxed they ever made under Jackson.

Beauregard's army was spread out along a small creek to the north and east of Manassas. During the first half of the Civil War, the practice was for the Confederacy to name battles after the nearest man-made location, the Union after natural sites. The battle that began on July 21, 1861, therefore, was called the battle of Bull Run in the North, the battle of Manassas in the South.

Because the battle was fought close to Washington

This contemporary cartoon depicts the British journalist William H. Russell. He traveled from Washington in a two-horse carriage, with ample picnicking provisions, to a spot near the battlefield where he wrote a graphic report of the battle of Bull Run that highlighted many of the Union mistakes.

and because it was advertised so far in advance, many local citizens and government representatives actually came out to watch. A journalist described what he saw atop a hill overlooking the scene: "There were carriages and [other] vehicles drawn up as if they were attending a small country race. . . . In one was a lady with an opera-glass. In and around . . . others were legislators and politicians. There were also a few civilians on horseback." The spectators expected the battle to be an entertaining diversion in which the Union troops thrashed the Confederates in time to have them all home for dinner.

The generals may have taken events a little more

Beauregard and McDowell's armies clash at Bull Run. *(Library of Congress)*

seriously: for them, a battle meant a bloody fight. The Confederate general Beauregard planned to move his right against the Federal left, so he had more forces to the right. He had hoped to have Johnston's men come in on the Federal right flank, but they joined the main army. McDowell had the same basic tactical plan, but he moved first. Confederate lookouts spotted the move. Beauregard sent some reinforcements, but still held most of his men back for his own planned offensive. By midmorning, the Confederates were in real trouble, being steadily pushed back by the Federal advance.

Jackson heard the firing and, apparently without orders, moved his brigade—his men running in the July heat—toward the sound of the guns. A few years before,

Jackson had told a VMI graduate that "a battle always had the effect of brightening his faculties, and that he had always thought more clearly, rapidly, and with more satisfaction to himself in the heat of an engagement than at any other time." Jackson was anxious to see his first major battle in thirteen years.

Three other brigades also marched toward the sound of the guns. As they approached the fighting, the men in Jackson's brigade had to work their way through increasingly numerous groups of stragglers. About 11:30 AM, Jackson reached Henry House Hill, with a view of the battle a few hundred yards to the north. Jackson could have charged his men into the fight. However, the Confederate forces were clearly losing, so he elected to stop his men and create a rallying point. He had his men form a line of battle on the back side of the hill. There they would be able to fire from the protection of the woods. They could also take cover from Union fire and reload their own guns over the crest of the hill.

Bull Run showed some of Jackson's characteristics as a leader. He was willing to risk his men in combat and certainly willing to put them through hard marches in the rain or heat, but Jackson would not risk his men unless there was a goal to be gained. His troops realized this, and they had enormous confidence in him. His name would become revered throughout the Confederacy, a symbol of strong, courageous leadership and unswerving devotion to his cause.

It was also at Bull Run that Jackson and his brigade

Jackson standing firm on Henry House Hill, where he earned his famous nickname, "Stonewall." *(Museum of the Confederacy, Richmond)*

entered the history books. Brigadier General Barnard Bee, who had fought with Jackson in Mexico, was now senior officer of the force Jackson and his troops were supporting. He rode up to Jackson, exclaiming, "General, they are driving us [back]!" Jackson responded firmly, "Sir, we will give them the bayonet." Bee then rode back to his men. He pointed his sword towards Henry House Hill and shouted, "Look, men, there is Jackson standing like a stone wall! Let us determine to die here, and we will conquer! Follow me!" Bee had just created one of the most famous nicknames in military history. Just a few hours later, Barnard Bee was killed.

Johnston and Beauregard used Jackson's brigade as a foundation to create a strong defensive line, which eventually stopped the Federal advance. At one point, they benefited from the confusion caused by the fact that uniforms had not yet been standardized to the Union navy blue and Confederate gray or "butternut" brown. A Union officer refused to give his men permission to fire on a blue-clad unit, believing they were Union soldiers. They turned out to be a Confederate unit, and they had time to get off a very damaging volley of rifle fire.

By four in the afternoon, both Confederate senior commanders saw that the time was right for a counterattack. The attack sent the Federal units into retreat. The retreating Union soldiers soon mixed with fleeing civilian onlookers, many of whom had come out to watch what they thought would be the only battle of the war. Then, a well-placed Southern artillery round hit a supply wagon on the only bridge across Bull Run. The retreat became a rout, ending only when the soldiers reached the defenses of Washington. Instead of pushing "on to Richmond," as the Union rallying cry had called for, Union troops now made a hasty retreat. It took them just a few hours to get back to Washington, compared to the five days it had taken them to get to Manassas.

A few hours later, Dr. Hunter McGuire, Jackson's medical director throughout the war, was treating a minor wound Jackson had received at Bull Run when a Federal bullet clipped the middle finger of his left hand.

Confederate president Jefferson Davis with his generals. From left to right: Beauregard, Jackson, Davis, Jeb Stuart, and Johnston. *(West Point Museum)*

He had been shot while making a gesture he became known for: thrusting his arm to the sky, palm out. McGuire and Jackson saw Confederate President Jefferson Davis arrive and begin trying to rally what he thought were stragglers. Jackson had to explain to Davis that the Confederates had won. Jackson asked for 10,000 fresh men and said he could be in Washington the next day.

Davis, though he likely appreciated what he later came to realize was Jackson's characteristic aggressiveness, agreed with Johnston and Beauregard that pursuit would not be wise. The Confederate army was as disorganized in victory as the Federal army was in defeat. A few days later, the Confederates would advance to Centreville, where they would sit for the next eight

"MASTERLY INACTIVITY," OR SIX MONTHS ON THE POTOMAC.

The eight-month silence after Bull Run made some soldiers and politicians wonder if the battle had been a false start to the war. The slow-moving style of the new Union general, George McClellan, quickly became a subject for political cartoons. Here, McClellan and Beauregard are depicted exchanging stares across the Potomac, while their troops engage in a snowball fight. *(Library of Congress)*

months. Fortunately for them, the Federal army, renamed the Army of the Potomac and now under the command of George McClellan, would sit in Washington for the next eight months.

Jackson believed that inactivity was bad for the Confederates, that the Southern military would lose the momentum of victory and its fighting trim. He was determined to keep his men in fighting order, however. He kept them carefully drilled and busy. Jackson maintained a highly disciplined force, even (much to the consternation of his men) prohibiting liquor from their camps. He continued to lead by example, providing his soldiers with a model of religious piety and ascetic devotion to cause. His weaknesses, however, were similar to his strengths. His reticence could make for trouble with subordinates, and his lack of confidence in his own intellect led him to neglect the written reports required of commanders. He shirked this duty out of fear and discomfort, afraid to put pencil to paper and have what he thought of as his own inadequacy revealed. Jackson would eventually find trusted aides who could relieve him of this responsibility. In the meantime, he did his best to avoid the issue entirely.

On October 7, 1861, Jackson was promoted to major general. He was assigned to command the new military district of the Shenandoah Valley a few days later. On November 4, Jackson said good-bye to his men. He praised the efforts of the assembled brigade, now called the Stonewall Brigade, which had served under his command at Harpers Ferry and Bull Run: "You are the *First Brigade!* In the affections of your General; and I hope, by your future deeds and bearing, you will be handed down to posterity as the *First Brigade,* in this our Second War of Independence. Farewell!" With these words, Jackson rode away to his new assignment.

Stonewall in the Valley

In 1883, writer George Pond described the geography of the Shenandoah Valley and its strategic value to both the North and the South during the American Civil War:

> Its eastern wall is the lofty Blue Ridge; its western, the North Mountains, a part of the main chain of the Alleghenies. Since its main course is southwesterly, a Confederate army moving northward through it would at the same time draw nearer to Washington, whereas a Union advance southward would diverge from the straight course to Richmond. . . . a Confederate force crossing [the Potomac River] at the mouth of the Valley . . . would already be sixty miles north in rear of Washington . . . and one day's march through the Cumberland Valley would carry a body of Confederate horsemen among the peaceful farm lands of

A view of the Shenandoah Valley during Stonewall Jackson's campaign. *(Library of Congress)*

Pennsylvania. Beautiful to look upon, and so fertile . . . the Valley furnished from its abundant crops much of the substance of Lee's army.

Jackson was initially given virtually no troops to defend the Shenandoah Valley. He was expected to make do with the local militia there—part-time troops raised for the defense of their immediate area. The militia was made up of about 1,700 men. Jackson's first task was to increase their numbers. He began by calling for all state militia troops, which produced another 1,300 men. He petitioned for, and received, the command of his old Stonewall Brigade. An additional force of five thousand men from far southwest Virginia, under General William Loring, was also assigned to Jackson's command.

While Jackson waited for Loring's troops to arrive, he had a very welcome distraction from the war. His wife, Anna, arrived in Winchester for a visit. It was not uncommon then for women and children to travel with the military. Jackson was reluctant to give his men furlough (a leave of absence), which made bringing their families to visit all the more attractive. Anna's presence cheered the general immensely. They set up housekeeping in the town and even made a kind of social life, dining with the local Presbyterian minister and other community leaders. The couple was together for Christmas, which was a dreary time. The weather was bad, the troops were unhappy at being denied leave, and Jackson was concerned about food shortages. Most of all, he was anxious to get back to work.

In December 1861, Jackson planned a major expedition to Romney, a strategic Federal post northwest of Winchester. The march, starting on the first day of the new year, began well. The weather was unusually spring-like, but the next day the temperature dropped and it began to snow and sleet heavily. Strong winds added to the misery of the 8,000 men. Dirt roads, hardened from the cold, turned slippery in the storm. Food and supply wagons had trouble keeping up with the men. Jackson was reluctant to let them stop to cook food before continuing the march. He finally agreed to let them grab what they could carry from the trailing supply wagons and then rejoin the march. Jackson did not mean to be careless with his men's welfare. He just expected every-

Jackson's troops trudge through the sleet and snow on their advance to Romney.
(Museum of the Confederacy, Richmond)

one to share his devotion to the cause, devotion that for him outweighed material needs such as food or sleep.

One of the traits Jackson's soldiers remarked upon most was how little sleep their commander seemed to need. He seemed to be awake at all hours of the day and night, constantly planning attacks or movements, pacing the area, or riding out to the sentries on Little Sorrel.

In truth, Jackson probably got as much sleep as anyone else, but he did so mainly in the form of naps. He had the ability to nod off at once, no matter where he was—sometimes, subordinates were sorry to notice, while they were speaking to him. He napped under trees, leaned up against fence posts, anywhere he could snatch a few moments of rest.

The troops had to sleep outside, without tents. The morning after a particularly snowy night, the area where the troops slept looked like a cemetery, with snow covering the gravestones. When daylight came, one Confederate observed, "these mounds were burst asunder and live men popped out of them, as if a resurrection was in progress." Jackson gave no slack, not even to his old brigade, now commanded by Richard Brooke Garnett. One day he discovered the Stonewall Brigade by the side of a road, cooking a meal. Jackson demanded an explanation as to why the brigade was not marching. Garnett responded, "I have halted to let the men cook their rations." Jackson told him sharply, "There is no time for that." Garnett objected, telling Jackson, "It is impossible for the men to march farther without them." Jackson ordered the brigade to get back in motion, then added to Garnett, "I have never found anything impossible with this brigade."

These difficult conditions made for some tension in the ranks. Jackson had trouble getting his various units to move where and when he wanted them to go. Loring's men, not used to the tough pace Jackson set on marches, were particularly unhappy, and particularly prone to complain. Loring became one of the first of Jackson's subordinates to experience, and object to, what was one of the general's worst faults. Jackson was always very secretive about his plans, even with his senior subordinates. This frustrated them, particularly be-

General William Loring. *(Valentine Museum, Richmond)*

cause, however carefully Jackson planned, unforeseen circumstances might force them to adapt his orders in the heat of the moment. If they did not know Jackson's goals, they were handicapped in reaching them. Jackson, in turn, complained that Loring and his men rarely carried out their instructions in a timely manner.

By January 14, 1862, when Jackson's men finally reached Romney, the Union forces had withdrawn. Given the difficult nature of communication and travel during those times, these kinds of near misses were hardly unusual. Armies relied heavily on scouts to learn the movements of other troops, and the scouts had to cover great distances—often at extreme peril—to relay their observations. By the time they made their reports, situations could easily have changed. Jackson's fruitless march to Romney was a learning experience. Fortunately, the Confederates were at least able to seize massive amounts of supplies and military equipment. After a few days, Jackson decided to leave Loring and his men at Romney, while the rest of the troops would return to Winchester.

A month later, Jackson learned that Loring had complained directly to the government in Richmond about having to stay in the exposed and less comfortable position at Romney. The government agreed with Loring, and Jackson was ordered to withdraw him back to Winchester. Jackson obeyed the orders, and then submitted his resignation, writing to the Secretary of War: "With such interference in my command I cannot expect to be of much service in the field; and . . . respectfully request that the President will accept my resignation from the Army."

Jackson believed strongly in the chain of command. To the degree possible, he carried out the orders of those above him in the Confederate military, as well as what he felt was the will of God. In turn, he expected those below him to carry out his orders without question. A storm followed the news of his resignation. Powerful people, including the governor of Virginia and Joseph Johnston, Jackson's military superior, sought to persuade him not to leave. Jackson finally withdrew his resignation, and Loring was transferred to the western theater of war.

In March of 1862, Jackson's troops in Winchester were facing nearly ten times as many Federals, led by Nathaniel P. Banks and James Shields. The Federals were moving quickly south towards Jackson and his men from three directions.

By March 11, Banks had arrived within striking distance of Winchester. Jackson, though heavily outnumbered, wanted to fight. He called a meeting of his subordinate commanders to discuss plans of attack. The subordinates, including the commander of the Stonewall Brigade, Richard Garnett, opposed immediate attack. Jackson accepted the decision, especially when he learned that Banks's army was already six miles south of Winchester. Jackson's army would have to give chase and would likely lose the battle. Jackson may have been saved from disaster, but as he headed out of Winchester with his small army, he was overcome with feelings of defeat, leaving, as they were, without a fight.

Over the next ten days, the Confederates withdrew to Mt. Jackson, about forty miles south of Winchester, where they gained three regiments of militia in reinforcement. From there, Jackson moved his army twenty-five miles north to Strasburg (about twenty miles south of Winchester). They reached their destination in one day, on March 22. Marching twenty-five miles in a day was not unusual for Jackson's hardened soldiers. The mounted soldiers headed by Turner Ashby, Jackson's cavalry chief, had skirmished with Federals in Winchester that very afternoon. Ashby told Jackson that he could take Winchester the next day if he had one infantry regiment to support the effort.

The next morning Jackson sent four infantry companies to Ashby, where they immediately joined in the skirmishing. Arriving Federal reinforcements prompted

This portrait of Jackson depicts the general in one of his moments of legendary leadership at Winchester.

Ashby to order a retreat to high ground north of Kernstown, two miles south of Winchester. By 2:30 that afternoon, the Federals were steadily forcing back the Confederates. Then Jackson and the main Confederate force arrived. Though unhappy about Sunday battles— Jackson never liked to fight on the Sabbath—Jackson realized that even a day's delay would enable the Union troops to dig in and obtain reinforcements.

On Pritchard's Hill, just north of Kernstown, Federal cannons prevented a direct approach to the Union position. The Union troops appeared more vulnerable on their right, and a flanking move was always Jackson's preferred tactic. Jackson felt his men could easily take the high ground on the Federal right, turn the enemy lines, and wedge themselves between the Federals and Winchester. He was sure this would mean victory. A small two-regiment brigade, under Colonel Samuel Fulkerson, was assigned the responsibility for moving around the Union right. The bulk of the Stonewall brigade would support Fulkerson.

At 3:30 PM, Fulkerson headed north toward the Federal right. Federal artillery immediately started shelling the brigade. Confederate efforts grew confused. An hour later, the battle was fully underway. Confederate forces were meeting very determined resistance and making little progress. About thirty minutes later, one of Jackson's aides reported that they were not facing just a few Federal regiments as they had thought, but 10,000 Federals, a full division. Ashby's cavalry had estimated

Richard Garnett. *(Library of Congress)*

Union numbers in the area to be low. It is unclear how the mistake was made, but however it happened, the Federal force Jackson had learned about at Kernstown was only about a quarter of the actual number of Federal troops in the area.

Jackson recognized that it was no longer possible for him to win. His only goal was to hold on until dark and make an orderly withdrawal. But this was not to be. The Confederate left was gradually being pushed out of its position and their ammunition was almost gone.

About 5:00 PM, the Stonewall Brigade ran out of ammunition. Garnett could not reach Jackson, so an hour later he ordered his brigade to withdraw. Though a logical move for Garnett to make, it exposed Fulkerson and his troops. The Confederate line's withdrawal turned into a rout, the only such defeat in Jackson's career. The best the reinforcing regiment Jackson sent could do was to cover the retreat. The Confederate forces went into a month-long withdrawal, ending up sixty miles south of Winchester. Anna Jackson and other family members visiting the troops had long since been sent home, out of harm's way. The camp was once again a collection of weary, battle-worn men, far from home or family and facing an uncertain future.

Jackson did not want his subordinates to act without orders and he was furious that Garnett had taken it upon himself to conduct a withdrawal. On April 1, 1862, Jackson had Garnett arrested and removed from command. A court-martial hearing was not convened until August. Jackson and one of his aides were the only witnesses slated to testify when the hearing was suspended as the second Bull Run campaign got under way. Garnett was soon restored to command, and served under James Longstreet at Antietam, Fredericksburg, and Gettysburg.

Though Jackson was revered by his troops, and soldiers throughout the Confederacy saw him as the epitome of bravery and strong leadership, he had a contentious relationship with most of his immediate staff. He was also hard on his troops, never hesitating to charge them with crimes of disobedience or insubordination. Garnett was only one of the many who experienced Jackson's harsh and unforgiving sense of justice. It seems Jackson saw no other option but to hold his troops to the same high standards to which he held himself, and he could not bear to be disappointed.

Kernstown turned out to be a strategic success, though Jackson clearly did not realize this at the time. The Federals sent twenty thousand more troops into the

Shenandoah Valley to chase Jackson. Since some of these were taken from the defenses of Washington, D.C., Lincoln personally borrowed men from the army George McClellan was assembling for his move on Richmond. This sapped the strength of the Union army and offered the Confederates a psychological advantage: McClellan had always assumed he was outnumbered, but now he thought he was outnumbered by even more men than before.

Now that Jackson was being chased into the valley, he put his analytical mind to work on the problem. Any good commander understands the importance of knowing the terrain he has to work with. Jackson brought into his service Major Jedediah Hotchkiss, a former teacher who was a self-taught engineer and mapmaker.

Jackson sent for Hotchkiss on March 26, 1862, during the retreat from Kernstown. Jackson's instructions were simple: "I want you to make me a map of the Valley, from Harper's [sic] Ferry to Lexington, showing all points of offense and defense in those places." Very few maps existed of the United States at that time, even fewer with military value. Because of this, military forces in the Civil War sometimes got lost, simply failing to show up when they were needed for an attack or defense. Familiarity with the ground in the Shenandoah Valley would give Jackson a major advantage over his Union opponents.

Particularly important would be familiarity with the Massanutten Mountain, a fifty-mile-long ridge that runs

This map of the Shenandoah Valley, edged by tough ridges and formidable gaps, gives an idea of the variety of terrain with which Jackson became intimately familiar during his campaign.

more or less north to south and divides the middle third of the valley in half. Roads ran parallel to the mountain on the eastern and western sides, and connecting roads crossed the ridge at the northern and southern edges. Most importantly, only one road crossed the ridge in the middle, from New Market on the west to Luray on the east. Jackson's army held New Market. He realized that if he controlled the road there, he could easily shift his troops back and forth over the mountain while his enemy would have to take a far longer route around the north or south.

Nathaniel Banks was the Union general sent into the

valley after Jackson. He spent the first half of April moving slowly south towards Jackson's position. Banks overestimated Jackson's strength and seemed not to know much about the valley—certainly no one had made him a map. Rain-swollen streams further delayed his approach.

Jackson, knowing Banks had nearly three times more men than he did, decided to try to avoid a confrontation. The Confederates withdrew further south but stayed where they could threaten the flank of any Union advance. Banks soon lost track of Jackson's force and assumed the troops had left the valley. He suggested to the government in Washington that his force could be withdrawn, either to join McClellan in the campaign

A page from the field sketchbook that Jedediah Hotchkiss used to map the valley for Jackson.

against Richmond or the Federal force between Richmond and Washington. The government took Banks's suggestion, planning to withdraw the bulk of his forces but leaving him with some men in the valley.

Robert E. Lee, then serving as military advisor to Confederate president Jefferson Davis, sent a letter to Jackson with some suggestions for a campaign. In doing so, Lee bypassed Jackson's direct superior, Joseph Johnston. Lee suggested that Jackson, reinforced by a division under Richard Ewell, should attack Banks's forces at Harrisonburg. Banks still heavily outnumbered Jackson as his men had not yet been removed. Jackson suggested an alternative to Lee's plan. He would join a small division under Edward Johnson in the western part of the state and attack the advance guard of another Federal force in the area, this one under

Union general Nathaniel Banks. (*Library of Congress*)

John C. Fremont. After Fremont's force had been pushed back, Jackson would take Johnson and Ewell and go after Banks. Lee gave his approval to the plan.

Jackson began his campaign in an unusual manner: by marching his men east, out of the Shenandoah Valley. He then put them on railroad cars and moved them back to the western valley to meet up with Johnson. (Jackson's men eventually came to assume that they were never going where they initially seemed to be headed.) Fremont was forced back as planned.

Banks's force was now down to eight thousand men,

so he began withdrawing north. Jackson had ten thousand men in his direct command, and Ewell had seven thousand. Ewell, though, was still under Joseph Johnston's direct command, and Johnston ordered Ewell to leave the valley and come to Richmond to help defend against McClellan's huge army. Jackson, always such a stickler for obeying the chain of command, violated his own principles by taking matters into his own hands.

On May 20, 1862, Jackson wrote Lee, asking if Johnston's orders could be changed: "I am of the opinion that an attempt should be made to defeat Banks, but under instructions just received from General Johnston, I do not feel at liberty to make an attack. Please answer by telegraph at once." He used a copy of Johnston's order to write to Ewell: "Suspend the execution of the order for returning to the east until I receive an answer to my telegraph." A clash between commanders was averted when Johnston wrote to Ewell, offering to re-

This letter from Johnston to Jackson gives Jackson and Ewell permission to join forces to fight Banks's troops in the Shenandoah Valley.

lease him from his orders: "The whole question is whether or not General Jackson and yourself are too late to attack Banks. If so, the march eastward should be made. If not (supposing your strength sufficient) then attack."

Jackson then cut through the Massanutten Mountain to hook up with Ewell. The combined forces attacked and virtually destroyed a small Federal force at Front Royal. Banks was shocked when he heard the reports of the battle; his most recent information put Jackson far away from the scene. It took Banks almost a full day to

Jackson is welcomed with cheers in Winchester after chasing Union forces out of town. *(Valentine Museum, Richmond)*

realize what Jackson had done and how quickly, by which time Jackson was preparing to attack Banks. Banks retreated to Winchester to make a stand, but a battle on May 25 forced him out of the town. The next day, Banks's forces retreated across the Potomac into Maryland.

Jackson hung around the northern valley for a few days to make sure Banks was out of the picture and to give his men as much rest as possible. From Washington, Abraham Lincoln saw an opportunity: he thought Jackson could be cut off and destroyed, and he knew the Federals had the men to do it. Fremont had fifteen thousand soldiers in western Virginia. A forty-mile march would put them on Jackson's supply lines, and cut him off from the south. Another forty thousand Union troops were at Fredericksburg. It would only take a day or two, Lincoln thought, for twenty thousand to head to Front Royal. The question was whether they could move fast enough.

Jackson had learned more in his time in battle than just the stubborn refusal to retreat that he had demonstrated while standing as firm as a stone wall at Bull Run. Within five days, he had moved his forces south of what Lincoln thought were the closing Federal pincers. The Union troops, not known for their speed at this point in the war, made doing this easy. For unknown reasons, Fremont marched north instead of directly east, making it harder for his men to block Jackson's movement. Fremont's prewar western explorations had earned him the nickname of "pathfinder." Escapades like this earned Fremont the nickname of the "lost pathfinder."

After some bad intelligence led them astray, Fremont's Mountain Department crossed the North Fork of the Shenandoah River in pursuit of Jackson. *(Library of Congress)*

Fremont did get turned around, eventually. His forces went after Jackson, who had headed farther south to Port Republic. On Sunday, June 8, Fremont's lead division, under James Shields, approached Port Republic. Jackson preferred not to fight on Sundays whenever it could be avoided. However, when a regiment of Shields's cavalry captured the key crossroads at Port Republic, Jackson had no choice. He personally organized the attack that threw the cavalry out. Not far away, at Cross Keys, Ewell was able to fight off an attack by Fremont's main forces. The next day, in a larger fight, the battle of Port Republic, Jackson's men defeated Shields and forced him back from Port Republic.

Jackson's leadership in the Shenandoah Valley made

him almost instantly famous in both Confederate and Union circles. The question now was what the general should do next. Happy news had recently arrived from home: Anna Jackson had written to her husband that she was pregnant. But Stonewall could not be with his wife during this time—instead he was called to Richmond for a conference. There it was decided that Jackson's army would be moved to join with Lee in the direct defense of Richmond, the Confederate capital.

By late May of 1862, McClellan and his Union army had almost reached the gates of Richmond. Joseph Johnston, commanding Confederate forces in Virginia, had withdrawn from Northern Virginia almost as far back as Richmond. Strategic retreat was always difficult, but with the Federals only six miles from Richmond, strategic withdrawal was no longer an option.

On May 31, 1862, Johnston attacked two Federal corps south of the rain-swollen Chickahominy River. Johnston was badly wounded in the battle and had to turn over command to the next senior officer, G. W. Smith. Smith continued the attack the next day, but managed to be driven back to the Confederate starting position. The evening of June 1, at the end of the battle, Jefferson Davis rode out to visit Smith and the wounded Johnston. Davis took his chief military advisor with him, Robert E. Lee. Smith seemed to be buckling under the pressure of being in charge. After some quiet thought, Davis gave Lee command of the army. Smith was removed, left the army, and faded from history. Lee imme-

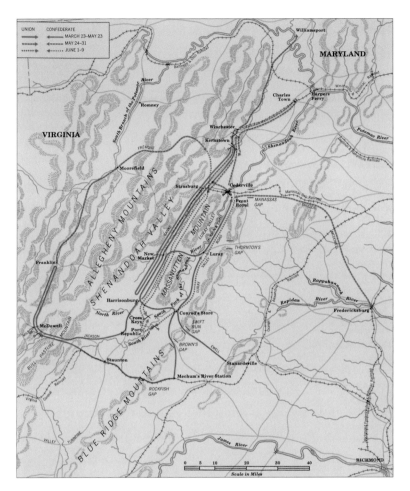

A map of the Shenandoah Valley showing Union and Confederate movement from March through early June, 1862.

diately renamed his army the Army of Northern Virginia, a name meant to inspire his troops to retake that land.

Lee's first objective was to get McClellan away from Richmond. Despite losing or stalemating most of the series of battles that followed, known as the Seven Days campaign, Lee managed to force McClellan back to the area of Fort Monroe, at the tip of the Virginia peninsula. Jackson and his men, though assigned to Lee, contributed very little to these battles: they were late for several attacks. In one case, the June 29 battle of Savage's Station, Jackson's men failed to show up at all. They had been delayed rebuilding some bridges. In other cases, they were late because the troops simply were not able to go as fast as they needed to over difficult terrain. Still other times, Jackson was given incorrect instructions or not told how urgent his moves were.

Still, the faltering of this normally stalwart general was puzzling. The most likely explanations offered for Jackson's struggle were that he was exhausted from the Shenandoah campaign, that the terrain he and his men faced was difficult to traverse, that he lacked Jedediah Hotchkiss's maps and the knowledge of the land they provided, and that the Confederate army in general had not yet developed a smooth system of coordination.

Jackson managed to recuperate during the relative quiet of July, 1862. At one point, he proposed an invasion of the North to Lee, and when Lee did not respond, to Jefferson Davis. But those plans had to be put on hold; a new problem was arising in Virginia.

Return to Bull Run

Even before the end of the Seven Days campaign, the Union put together a second main army, the Army of Virginia, under John Pope, to operate in Northern Virginia. Pope's army joined the units under McDowell with Jackson's old foes, Fremont and Banks. The army was designed to operate in northern Virginia, in cooperation with McClellan's operations near Richmond. The Federal high command intended for Pope's army to force Lee to redirect some of the troops watching McClellan. This would actually happen but not in the way the Union intended.

Jackson, always an aggressive commander, was thinking along different lines. Early in July, he was speaking with a friend who was also a Confederate congressman. Jackson told his friend, "Do you know we are losing valuable time there?" The congressman asked how. Jackson continued, "Why, by repeating the blunder we made after the battle of Manassas, in allowing the enemy leisure to recover from his defeat and ourselves to suffer by inaction." Jackson was trying to convince President Davis and General Lee to approve an invasion of the North, to dramatically shift the initiative to the Confederates. A successful invasion of the North might encourage popular pressure on the Northern government to make peace. But there remained the problem of Pope's army.

On July 13, 1862, McClellan was still inactive in camp near Fort Monroe. He seemed likely to remain that way for a while, so Lee needed fewer men to monitor his army's doings. Lee sent Jackson and ten thousand men to Gordonsville, fifty miles northwest of Richmond. The next few weeks were quiet, which gave Jackson a chance to rest and resupply his men. He also had the chance to pursue courts-martial against some subordinate officers, including Richard Garnett, former commander of the Stonewall Brigade.

Despite his military skills, Jackson was never a good administrator. He set very high standards, and had problems adjusting to different levels of ability and understanding among people. This had likely been a cause of his one-size-fits-all teaching style at VMI. There Jackson had assumed that all students could understand a lesson after one or two repetitions of the basic material. Jackson now assumed that his military subordinates not

Union general George McClellan. *(National Portrait Gallery, Washington, D.C.)*

only thought the way he did, but also had his leadership skills and his ability to concentrate on the task at hand. They were as capable of obeying orders from higher-ups as he was, and they should be able to carry out those orders just as well. When this did not happen, or when his officers improvised, he saw their behavior as intentional insubordination. A court-martial (a military trial) would frequently follow. Jackson also had no tolerance for deserters from his army—he invariably ordered death sentences for any men caught trying to escape their service. Though it was clear to those who knew him that Jackson hated to see his own men shot to death, he did not hesitate to do what he believed was necessary for the good of his army.

Union general John Pope. *(Library of Congress)*

By August, the Confederate command realized that the Lincoln administration was withdrawing units from McClellan's army and shipping them to Pope. This meant that Pope's would likely be the main Union army in Virginia. The Confederates also had reports that Pope had added a new ele-

General Pope's headquarters at Rappahannock Station, Virginia. *(Library of Congress)*

ment to the war by taking direct actions against civilians. Involving civilians represented a significant shift in the conduct of the war.

Three general orders, issued July 18, 1862, described the measures Pope planned to use to keep the citizens of occupied Virginia territory under strict control. The Army of Virginia would live off the land, to the extent possible, and would pay for whatever remaining supplies it needed with vouchers. These vouchers could be redeemed at the war's end, but only if the owner could prove having been a loyal citizen of the United States (meaning not a Confederate supporter) since the date of the voucher. It was unclear how this proof could be offered. In practice, this meant citizens had their resources confiscated with little hope of remuneration.

Further, Southern citizens would be held responsible for damage to Federal railroad tracks, telegraph lines, and roads, and for attacks on army supply convoys. Payment would be made by personally repairing the damage and paying, in money or property, the expenses of Federal troops enforcing these measures. Any person whose house was used to fire on Federal troops would have their house burned and be arrested. Anyone caught firing on Federal troops would be shot.

These policies were met with anger and fear in the South, and sentiment among civilians as well as military leaders was that Pope had not just to be defeated but suppressed. Jackson, reinforced to twenty-eight thousand men, was to start doing the suppressing. On August 7, Jackson got word that part of Pope's army, under Banks, had advanced to Culpeper Court House, twenty-five miles from Gordonsville. It took Jackson's men two days to get to Culpeper.

Jackson's habit of keeping his plans to himself, not even sharing them with his senior subordinates, delayed progress. But lax security was a frequent problem in the Civil War, and Jackson was not the only general to be concerned about the enemy learning his plans. Federal commanders were plagued by their intentions being broadcast in Northern newspapers. Southern generals, including Lee, regularly read these papers.

Secretiveness, in itself, was not a bad way of keeping plans from leaking, but Jackson sometimes overdid it. He tended not to give his subordinates enough information to carry out the spirit as well as the letter of his orders. His men learned to live with difficult marches in good and bad weather, usually not knowing their end point. This situation created problems for his division commanders who, not knowing their destination, had a difficult time responding to the inevitable obstacles that interrupted their path. Even when secrecy was not intended, Civil War staff work, particularly the transmission of orders, was often carried out in an inefficient manner.

One of Jackson's division commanders later complained that it was Jackson's habit to send them to one point where they would meet a staff officer who would tell them where to go next. Problems arose when meetings were delayed or missed. Even Robert E. Lee, in late July, had suggested in a letter to Jackson that "by advising your division commanders much trouble will be saved you in arranging details so they can act more intelligently." Jackson did not take the hint and remained as secretive as ever.

Jackson believed strongly in the chain of command: that soldiers did not question orders. Being very religious, Jackson considered God as the top of the command chain. His characteristic resolution came from his conviction that God had ordained events in the war, and that all the soldiers needed to do was carry out their duties.

Jackson wanted war to be as orderly and organized as possible. Delays, even those caused by his own policies, annoyed him. But despite delays, and even though the Union commanders knew Jackson and his men were coming, Jackson felt little concern about what lay ahead. He would again be facing Nathaniel Banks, who had not done well in the Shenandoah Valley. Jackson remarked to an aide riding with him, "Banks is in our front, and he is generally willing to fight. And he generally gets whipped."

Jackson's units were still spread out on the road when he found Banks near a hill named Cedar Mountain on August 9, 1862. Though his army was not yet fully assembled, Jackson had his leading units attack. Much to Jackson's surprise, Banks's men put up a stiff resistance. The Confederate attack was going nowhere. In the early evening, Banks managed to get a force around Jackson's left. Jackson's official report stated that the attack "fell with great vigor upon our extreme left, and by the force of superior numbers, bearing down all opposition, turned it and poured a destructive fire into its rear." Some of Jackson's men broke. Had Banks sent a larger force, he might have won a significant victory.

Jackson rode into the fray in an attempt to rally his men. The line began to stabilize, but it was still touch and go. Then A. P. Hill arrived with the first of his units. Hill's men succeeded in turning around the battle and sending Banks's corps into retreat. Later, historians would criticize Jackson for not having performed up to his usual level at Cedar Mountain, for attacking before all his men were on hand when he might have waited, and for failing to destroy a smaller force led by a poor general. But Cedar Mountain was, in the end, a Southern victory that improved morale for a far larger battle to follow. The battle also solidified Jackson's reputation among his soldiers as a fearless leader. His psychological impor-

Even though the battle at Cedar Mountain was a victory for the Confederacy, it was extremely costly in terms of human lives. *(Library of Congress)*

tance to the troops cannot be overstated: when Jackson rode into a camp, one witness reported, "I thought the heavens would have been rent with the cheers!" As another soldier remembered, "Jackson usually is an indifferent and slouchy looking man but then, with the 'Light of Battle' shedding its radiance over him his whole person had changed. . . . The men would have followed him into the jaws of death itself." At Cedar Mountain, death was not far away; the fight lasted only an hour and a half but saw nearly three thousand men killed.

About a week later, Lee learned that McClellan's divisions were being taken from his camp near Fort Monroe and sent to join Pope. Lee decided to act before Pope's army could be heavily reinforced. He spent about ten days maneuvering before deciding on a more daring plan. Jackson would make a wide turning movement around Pope's western flank. Lee hoped that even if he could not bring Pope to battle, the move would force Pope to withdraw to cover his lines of communication to Washington. This would increase the distance

Commander of the Confederate forces, General Robert E. Lee. *(Virginia Historical Society, Richmond)*

McClellan's units had to travel to link up with Pope.

Lee was somewhat nervous about putting Jackson in charge of such an important maneuver. He knew Jackson only very little, and while Confederate soldiers greeted his name with cheers, Jackson had not done anything particularly remarkable since he confounded Banks in the Shenandoah Valley. Jackson's standoffish personality did little to invoke confidence, nor did his slightly unusual background. Lee and most of his immediate subordinates had served together in the army since the Mexican War. Jackson had spent many of the years between the Mexican War and the Civil War teaching. No one was quite sure what to expect from him. Still, when Lee gave Jackson his orders, the latter gathered his forces and left camp without a moment's delay.

Jackson's troops headed quickly to the northwest. His move was actually spotted by Federal cavalry, but Pope assumed Jackson was headed back to his old stomping grounds, the Shenandoah Valley. Confederate general James Longstreet had also been ordered into the area and was moving his forces around to convince Pope that he might be attacking, thus keeping Pope's army in place.

August 26 saw Jackson's forces reach Bristoe Station, directly on Pope's supply lines. Three Federal supply trains were the first to see the Confederate troops. The first train's engineer spotted them in time to back safely away. The second train was derailed, but the third also managed to escape. The telegraph line between Pope's headquarters and Washington went dead that evening. The next morning, Federal scouts told Pope what he already suspected: a large Confederate force had managed to sneak into position behind him.

Three days of tense maneuvering began. Jackson was in a dangerous position, with fewer men than Pope and cut off from easy support by Lee. Pope did not know exactly where Jackson was, but he nonetheless began to move in Jackson's approximate direction. Jackson left one division at Bristoe Station and moved the other two to Manassas Junction, not far from Manassas. There Jackson captured a large Federal supply depot. When he realized he could not remain in control of the depot, he permitted his men to take what they wanted, except for alcohol. The depot was then burned.

Jackson then moved his men to Groveton, a small village near the Bull Run battlefield, where he had earned his nickname thirteen months earlier. On August 28, Jackson placed his men out of sight in a slight ditch, in an unfinished railroad spur. Late that afternoon, a Federal division headed by Rufus King passed by on its way to Manassas, about ten miles away, where they thought Jackson could be found. Jackson decided to attack. He wanted to draw Pope into the open, to keep him vulnerable to an attack by the rest of Lee's army.

Trying to determine whether his attack would work, Jackson rode out about a quarter mile in front of his men, parallel to the Union troops, and trotted back and forth studying them. His men watched nervously. Somehow, the Federal troops managed not to notice Jackson, or they saw him and did not consider him important enough to shoot. Jackson's habit of never dressing like an important general had its advantages.

Returning to his lines, Jackson ordered the attack to start. Two and a half hours of hard fighting between Ewell's Confederate division and Rufus King's Federal troops ensued. The fighting ended more or less in a stalemate, though King's division ultimately withdrew. Strategically, however, Jackson achieved his goal. Pope was drawn out into the open to attack Jackson, not realizing that Lee and the rest of his army were on their way.

Jackson's force was still at Groveton on August 29. That morning, Pope began to move into position, beginning his attack in the afternoon. Jackson's men fought hard. When ammunition ran out, some threw stones at the attacking Federals. At one point, one of A. P. Hill's brigade commanders informed Hill, "my ammunition is exhausted, but . . . I will hold my posi-

General A. P. Hill. *(Library of Congress)*

tion with the bayonet." Hill sent a courier to inform Jackson he was not sure his men could hold. Jackson sent the courier back with a message for Hill, "Tell him that if they are attacked he must beat them back!" Jackson then rode after the courier to tell Hill personally, "Your men have done nobly. If you are attacked again you will beat the enemy back." His certainty never wavered.

Before Hill could respond, he heard gunfire from his lines and rode off to check on them. Jackson called after him, "I'll expect you to beat them." Hill's men did beat them. An aide to one of his brigade commanders later said, "We slaughtered them like hogs. I never saw the like of dead men in all my life." When notified of Hill's success, Jackson told Hill's aide, "Tell him I knew he could do it."

Lee, James Longstreet, and the rest of the Army of Northern Virginia arrived that afternoon, coming in on Jackson's right, but remaining concealed. Longstreet wanted to hold off on an immediate attack, unless Jackson needed help, to see what forces Pope would bring and also to find the moment when an attack would do the most damage to the Federals.

The next morning, August 30, Pope was still not aware that he was facing all of Lee's army. When he attacked Jackson, Longstreet's artillery helped fight off the attack. After a couple of hours, Longstreet decided the time was right. His corps smashed into Pope's right flank, forcing Pope back. As fate would have it, the

Federals managed to avoid a rout by making a stand on Henry House Hill, where Jackson and his men had stood their ground a year earlier. The Federals then withdrew in the direction of Washington, D.C., but in much better order this time than the year before.

Heavy rain that night gave the Federals a head start. But this time Jackson was able to go after them. The next day, when the weather cleared up, Jackson took his corps northward, to try to get around the Federal left flank. Unbeknownst to Lee, a Union sympathizer had reported this plan to Pope. The Union divisions under Philip Kearney, one of the best Federal commanders, and Isaac Stevens, were sent to intercept.

They caught up with the Confederates near Ox Hill and the small village of Chantilly on September 1. When the Confederates got word of the Union advance, they turned south and moved through the woods just below the Little River Turnpike. The rain was as hard as it had been two days before. The soldiers complained as much as always, but still did what Jackson asked.

As they moved south, the Confederates met Federal guns. Jackson opted to fully turn his divisions to meet this threat. He described the battle in a report written in late April 1863:

> Late in the evening, after reaching Ox Hill [we] came in contact with the enemy . . . in position on our right and front, covering his line of retreat from Centreville to Fairfax Court House. Our line of battle was formed . . . all on the right of the turnpike road. Artillery was

posted on an eminence to the left of the road. ... [Two brigades] were sent forward to feel and engage the enemy. A cold and drenching thunderstorm swept over the field at this time, striking directly into the faces of our troops. These two brigades gallantly engaged the enemy, but so severe was the fire in front and flank of Branch's brigade as to produce some disorder ... the conflict now raged with great fury, the enemy obstinately and desperately contested the field."

General Stevens's Union division was not fully into position until that afternoon, and Stevens was killed leading the charge that followed. The Confederates began to fall back when it again started to rain heavily. Another distinguished Union general, General Philip Kearny, was also killed on this day. As the fighting wore on, Kearny's passions were stirred and he rode directly into Jackson's firing troops, perhaps unintentionally.

The increasingly severe thunderstorm, along with the deaths of the two ranking Federal commanders, ended the battle. The Union troops withdrew back to Washington and the Confederates pulled back to prepare for their next move.

7

Invading the North

The triumph of the Shenandoah campaign had shifted the balance of power to the Confederacy. Robert E. Lee now had to decide how to use this advantage. He opted to do what Jackson had suggested some six weeks earlier: to send the Army of Northern Virginia into Maryland. Lee wrote Confederate president Jefferson Davis about the proposed invasion:

> The present seems to be the most propitious time since the commencement of the war for the Confederate Army to enter Maryland. The two grand armies of the United States that have been operating in Virginia, though now united, are much weakened and demoralized. Their new levies, of which I understand 60,000 men have already been posted in Washington, are not yet organized, and will take some time to

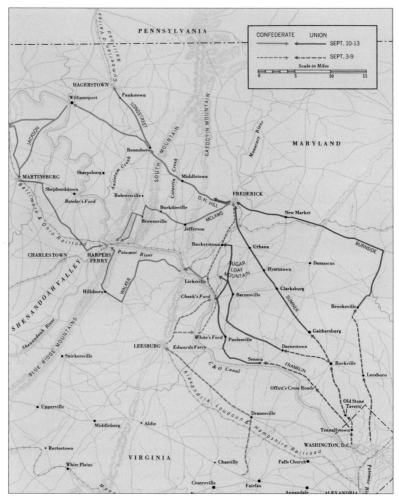

The Confederate and Union movements in Maryland in the early fall of 1862.

prepare for the field. If it is ever desired to give material aid to Maryland and afford her an opportunity of throwing off the oppression to which she is now subject, this would seem the most favorable.

Lee conceded there were many logistical and supply problems, and a particularly severe manpower shortage, that he would face in the incursion, but argued against a static defense. Like Jackson, Lee wanted to keep Confederate momentum going.

There were risks, but Lee considered them worth taking. The proposed campaign would defend Richmond by drawing the main Federal army far away from the Confederate capital. Northern Virginia would get a respite from the constant strife it had been enduring. Lee's army could have access to fresh supplies from untouched territory in the northern part of the state. Lee thought his offensive might fuel pro-Confederate sentiment in Maryland—currently western Maryland was pro-Union, while the eastern part of the state supported the Confederacy. Finally, a successful Confederate offensive in the east coupled with plans for a near simultaneous advance by Southern armies in the west into Kentucky and Ohio, might convince European leaders to recognize the Confederacy. At the very least, a successful invasion of northern soil would hurt the Republicans in the 1862 elections, only two months away.

Lee could not have known another reason favoring invasion of the North. Lincoln's issuance of the Emancipation Proclamation, which would free slaves in Confederate territory, was on hold. His cabinet wanted to wait to release it until the Union troops could win a victory. A major Union defeat, on Union territory, at the very least would postpone the Proclamation's issuance.

A Confederate defeat, however, or even the destruction of Lee's army, was possible and would be a major disaster for the South. Lee later responded to concerns about the great risk he had taken: "Such criticisms were obvious, but that the disparity of forces between the contending armies rendered the risks unavoidable."

Lee's army began moving into Maryland at White's Ford, on September 4, 1862, taking three days to get across the river. Lee rode in an ambulance, having injured both his hands on the last day of August. He could not mount his horse. Jackson had hurt himself falling off a horse, so he also had to enter Maryland riding in an ambulance. Lee crossed the Potomac with roughly fifty-five thousand men, but these numbers quickly began to decline. Many, even most, soldiers in the Civil War had enlisted to defend their homes and

Union scouts watched as Lee's army crossed the Potomac River at White's Ford. News of the crossing stunned Federal officials in Washington, who were completely unprepared for the Confederate invasion. *(Library of Congress)*

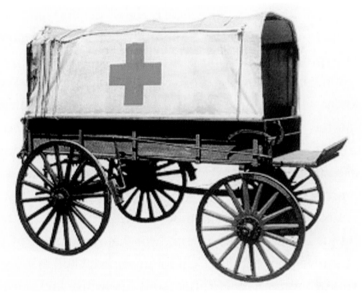

A Civil War-era ambulance.

local areas. They had not signed up to invade the North. Homesickness, uncertainty, and the privations they had endured proved to be too much; as the army approached Maryland, soldiers began to desert. Lee entered Maryland with only forty thousand soldiers, the weakest numbers he had yet commanded.

Jackson was, as usual, convinced that the march was not up to his standards for speed and order. At one point, riding up and down his lines to ensure proper progress, he found that a brigade of A. P. Hill's division was not on the road when it was supposed to be. Jackson could not find Hill, but found the brigade commander. Jackson wanted to know why the brigade was not marching. The commander, Brigadier General Maxcy Gregg, said they were filling their canteens with water. Jackson then snapped loudly, so the nearly deaf general and those around him could hear, "There are but few commanders who properly appreciate the value of celerity!"

On September 2, 1862, the Union abolished Pope's Army of Virginia and his troops were reincorporated into the Army of the Potomac. George McClellan was put in charge of the Washington, D.C. defenses and would also command the Army of the Potomac against Lee's approaching forces.

Late on Friday, September 5, McClellan began moving his troops northwest into Maryland in pursuit of Lee. On September 9, 1862, gambling on McClellan's typical lack of aggressiveness, Lee split his army. Jackson took roughly half the men to Harpers Ferry in an effort to capture the fort and detain the nearly thirteen thousand Union soldiers there. Securing the area was crucial to keeping Lee's route accessible.

Early in the evening of September 10, a small Union cavalry patrol from Harpers Ferry was out investigating a rumor that Confederates had been spotted near Boonsboro, Maryland, about fifteen miles north of Harpers Ferry. Riding down the main street of town, the patrol ran into some Confederates, the advance element of Jackson's command. The Union cavalrymen charged, sending the surprised Confederates retreating in the direction of the main body of troops. To their surprise, they soon ran into Jackson himself, walking calmly down the road. Apparently just seeing Jackson was motivation enough for the retreating Confederates. They

Union soldiers survey Harpers Ferry from an outpost at Maryland Heights. *(Corcoran Gallery, Washington, D.C.)*

turned on the Union troops and forced them back.

The Union commander reported what he had seen to Colonel Dixon Miles, who was in charge of the Harpers Ferry garrison. Miles then telegraphed Washington: "Enemy reported in Boonesborough. . . . He may intend to pass on to Maryland Heights or the Potomac at Antietam Creek. Troops in position and ready."

Thursday, September 11, Jackson's forces crossed the Potomac upriver at Williamsport. The Confederates quickly cut off all but one line of retreat for a smaller Federal garrison at Martinsburg, which retreated to Harpers Ferry. At the same time, a two-division Confederate force was headed towards Maryland Heights, under orders to take the heights by the next morning. A third

Confederate force would approach the town from the Virginia side of the Potomac, toward Loudon Heights. Thus Harpers Ferry would be virtually surrounded and pinned down from superior positions. Fortunately for Jackson's men, the weather was good. They still griped about the rapid marches and never knowing their destination, but they also had faith that Jackson knew what he was doing.

Skirmishing began at Maryland Heights the evening of September 11. Just before midnight, Miles sent his last message to Washington, reporting on the start of the battle. The next morning, the two leading Confederate brigades began to climb the heights on the sloping northern side. Federal reinforcements were sent, but the Confederates forced them off the next day. Union retreat

This photograph, taken by famed Civil War photographer Matthew Brady, shows the town of Harpers Ferry after it was shelled by Lee's army and the railroad bridge was destroyed. *(Library of Congress)*

to the North was cut off. The Confederates began to shell Harpers Ferry. The town was also shelled from Loudon Heights to the east and Bolivar Heights to the west and south. The town and garrison were surrendered on September 15, before Jackson's major infantry attack had even begun.

Jackson had taken his men to Harpers Ferry in accordance with Lee's Special Orders No. 191, which detailed the positions and planned movements of all elements of the Army of Northern Virginia. Lee wrote out the orders and distributed copies to each of the eight generals under his command. Unfortunately for the Confederates, one of the copies of Special Orders No. 191 was lost. Union soldiers soon found the copy of the orders in an abandoned Confederate camp, wrapped around three cigars.

The soldiers first noticed the cigars, but then noticed the wrapper. They took it to their company commander, who quickly sent the document up the chain of command. A senior staff officer in their division authenticated the document when he recognized the handwriting as belonging to a member of Lee's staff, a fellow soldier from the pre-war U.S. Army. He went to the commander of the Federal Twelfth Corp, who sent the documents on to McClellan. McClellan took one look at the document, and exclaimed, "Now I know what to do."

McClellan, a classmate of Jackson's at West Point, began to move quickly—though the Union general was still not known for his speediness. McClellan defeated part of Lee's army on September 14 in the battle of South Mountain, pushing the Confederate troops westward. The next morning Lee received a message from Jackson, sent via Jeb Stuart: "Through God's blessing, Harper's Ferry and its garrison are to be surrendered. As Hill's troops have borne the heaviest part in the engagement, he will be left in command until the prisoners and public property shall be disposed of, unless you direct otherwise. The other forces can move off this evening so soon as they get their rations. To what place shall they move?" Relieved by this good news, Lee ordered that, except for Hill's troops, the Army of Northern Virginia should reunite at Sharpsburg, Maryland, just north of the Potomac and seventeen miles northwest of Harpers Ferry. Jackson was alerted to this plan.

Lee's men began to arrive at Sharpsburg on September 15, though it would be another day before the bulk of the army arrived. The first Federal divisions arrived the same evening, taking up positions across Antietam Creek. Estimates are that by the morning of September 16, Lee had fifteen thousand men with him and faced nearly sixty thousand men immediately available to McClellan. More Union troops were on the way.

As a general, McClellan was almost the total opposite of Jackson and Lee. In keeping with his nature, McClellan took things slowly and carefully, spending the day studying Confederate positions and waiting for more of his men to arrive. Lee's position was strong, anchored on available high ground and Antietam Creek, but he had few men to hold the position and no place to retreat to in case of defeat. The Potomac River was less than two miles behind the Confederate lines, effectively pinning them in place.

Lee put on a bold front, bluffing McClellan into delaying the attack. Jackson arrived that day, with most of his men, but even with Jackson's troops, Lee only had at most thirty-five thousand men to fight off twice the amount of Federal troops in the immediate vicinity and even more within an easy march.

McClellan's plan was to attack on both the Confederate left and right while pretending to attack in the center. The attack in the center could become a full-fledged assault if the opportunity presented itself, if Lee weakened that area to defend his flanks. This was a good plan if carried out by an aggressive and resolute commander. But McClellan lacked such confidence. His report on the battle, written about a month later, shows a bit of this confusion: "The design was to make the main attack upon the enemy's left—at least to create a diversion in favor of the main attack, with the hope of something more by assailing the enemy's right—and, as soon as one or both of the flank movements were fully successful, to attack their center with any reserve I might then have on hand."

McClellan had the manpower to stage a coordinated attack and quickly finish off Lee's army. He had a plan that might have worked, that might have won the North an overwhelming victory. However, McClellan allowed

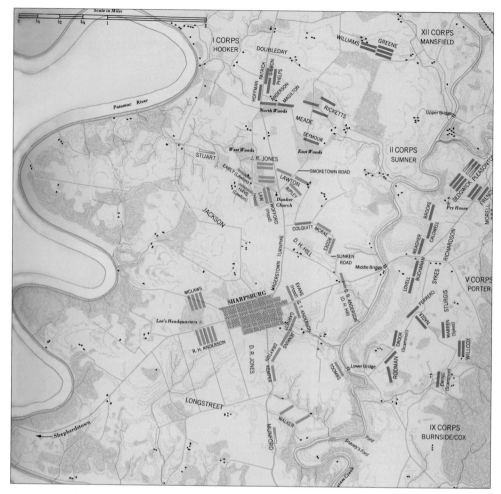

This map of the Antietam battlefield details the positions of the opposing armies at dawn on September 17, 1862. (Red=Confederate, Blue=Union)

his subordinates to attack one sector at a time, failing to coordinate Union efforts.

The bloodiest day in American military history, September 17, 1862, began about 6:00 AM General Joseph Hooker's First Corps of the Union army, having crossed Antietam Creek the evening before, struck against Stonewall Jackson's men on the Confederate left wing.

The first phase of the attack caused heavy damage to both of Jackson's divisions in the area. The evening before, Jackson had given John Bell Hood permission to move his division behind the lines so his men could cook rations and get some rest. Hood promised his men would return immediately when they were needed. When one phase of Hooker's attack came through a cornfield, Jackson called on Hood to keep his promise. Hood's men fiercely attacked Hooker's men in the cornfield. When the attack ended, Hood's division was as wrecked as Jackson's other units. But so were the Union forces, and the danger in this sector had passed. The cornfield had been completely cut down by gunfire.

Hard fighting continued for ninety minutes before Hooker received any Federal reinforcements. Portions of the Twelfth Corps were fed into action about 7:30 AM, not to exploit a breakthrough but to back up a generally wrecked First Corps.

The fighting on Jackson's sector of the Confederate line had been the heaviest he had encountered in the war so far, yet his men had held. About noon, as combat continued in the center, Dr. Hunter McGuire was talking with Jackson. He asked Jackson if the line could hold against another attack. Jackson responded, "I think they [the Union forces] have done their worst. There is now no danger of the line being broken."

The story was different in the center of the Confederate line. Union efforts against the Confederate center began almost by accident, when Jackson's old commander and nemesis from Florida, William French, had inadvertently led his Union troops into the Confederate line. The main element of the Southern position was a

This painting by James Hope shows a view of the sunken road, also known as Bloody Lane, filled with Confederate and Union dead.

sunken road, later known as Bloody Lane. Years of wagon traffic had dug out the road to about a foot below the nearby ground. The lane was hidden to advancing soldiers by a rise in the ground. When the Union troops passed over the rise, they would be very good targets as they were outlined against the morning sun.

Photographs taken a few days later show Bloody Lane covered with both Union and Confederate dead. Both sides suffered heavy losses, and the Confederate line was briefly broken. But the key Union general on the scene was killed, causing the Union some loss of momentum. Federal troops were ordered to hold their position, and Lee was given time to repair the break in his lines.

McClellan was later criticized for his failure to make a coordinated effort against all sectors of Lee's army, a failure that enabled Lee to shift his troops to where they were needed. However, even though he did not ensure that the attack was carried out, McClellan had in fact ordered an attack on the Confederate right at the same

One of the most famous photographs of the Civil War is this one of Bloody Lane, taken by Alexander Gardner. His photographs of the Antietam battle sites were the first ever of an American battlefield before the dead had been buried. *(Library of Congress)*

time his main attack opened against Jackson's position on the Confederate left.

Ambrose Burnside, commanding the Federal left, was supposed to create a diversion against the Confederate right to draw troops away from the main fight. But he had neglected to fully check the ground, and his troops were divided: one division was out looking for a shallow place to cross Antietam Creek. Though they eventually found one, most of Burnside's men were trying, with great difficulty, to cross over the one narrow bridge. It took them several hours to cross the creek and begin their main attack. By this time the rest of the fighting was over and the planned diversion had failed. But Burnside

Painter James Hope's portrayal of Union reinforcements crossing the bridge over Antietam Creek. *(Antietam National Battlefield, Sharpsburg, MD)*

(whose bushy facial hair gave rise to the term "sideburns") could not know this, and he ordered his men forward.

The attack initially went well, pushing back the Confederate right through the streets of Sharpsburg. About 4:30 PM, however, this changed when A. P. Hill's Confederate division showed up after a seventeen-mile march from Harpers Ferry. Hill finally learned Jackson's lesson about the need for a rapid march to battle. Though half his men were stragglers, enough remained to slam into Burnside's left flank, stopping its progress and forcing Union troops back across what became known as Burnside Bridge. McClellan then seemed to give up. No further attacks followed. Confederate General James Longstreet later wrote, "We were so badly crushed at the close of the day that ten thousand fresh troops could have come in and taken Lee's army and everything in it." But McClellan was apparently unaware of his advantage.

The fighting at Antietam was the fiercest and most costly of the war so far, and September 17, 1862 is known

This photograph, taken by Alexander Gardner on October 4, 1862, shows President Lincoln meeting with McClellan at his headquarters. *(Library of Congress)*

as the bloodiest single day of the entire war, with roughly twenty-three thousand dead and wounded, divided nearly evenly between the two sides. Though McClellan received at least twenty-five thousand fresh Union troops, he did not mount another attack at Antietam. The next day, September 18, 1862, he allowed Lee's decimated army to slip back over the Potomac.

Two significant results took place after the Antietam campaign. On November 7, 1862, McClellan was removed from command of the Army of the Potomac and Ambrose Burnside was put in command. The news was generally not taken well in the army, where McClellan was popular, but the good news was that Burnside was an appealingly modest commander in an era of difficult personalities. The bad news for the Union was that he was correct when he claimed he was not qualified to command an army, as he proved a month later in his mishandling of the battle of Fredericksburg.

The other, more important, result of the battle of Antietam was that Lincoln issued a preliminary Emancipation Proclamation on September 22, 1862. As of January 1, 1863, all slaves in areas still in rebellion would be free. Few slaves were actually freed—this would come later—but the proclamation put the North firmly on the side of freedom and against slavery. Compromise became impossible, and it was clear the war would have to be fought to the end. European recognition of the Confederacy and intervention to settle the war would now be far more difficult to win.

The best chance the Confederates had for outside aid was gone. Their only hope for winning the war lay in Lee's army. One dispatch, filed in late September by a

Lincoln's Emancipation Proclamation, issued formally on January 1, 1863, did little to immediately free the slaves. However, the document was invested with much symbolic power. *(Library of Congress)*

Confederate correspondent, declared, "The army in Virginia stands guard this day, as it will stand guard this winter, over every hearthstone throughout the South. The ragged sentinel who may pace his weary rounds this winter on the bleak spurs

Union general Ambrose Burnside. *(National Portrait Gallery, Washington, D.C.)*

of the Blue Ridge, or along the frozen valleys of the Shenandoah and Rappahannock, will also be your sentinel, my friend, at home." The determination and resolve Stonewall Jackson showed now became the conviction of every Confederate soldier. Yet these same soldiers were poorly outfitted and supplied, staring into the face of a long winter. Many did not have shoes, most went without blankets or tents, and all subsisted on what little food there was to be have from the ravaged land.

Two months later Ambrose Burnside made his first move as commander of the Army of the Potomac. He planned to cross the Rappahannock River from Fredericksburg, Virginia and attack Lee from behind. The first elements of the Army of the Potomac arrived on the shores of the river on November 17, 1862, with the bulk of the army arriving a few days later. Unfortunately, the Rappahannock was not fordable at that point under the best of circumstances. Heavy rains were making the river more impossible to cross. Pontoons, to be used to bridge the river, did not arrive until November 27, ten days later. The Union troops could only sit and wait.

On November 19, Lee had started moving his men towards Fredericksburg. Virtually all of his army was in place by November 24, three days before Burnside's army could start

Union general Joseph Hooker. *(National Portrait Gallery, Washington, D.C.)*

crossing. Burnside, his hope for a surprise gone, had to find another plan. In the end, he opted for a direct attack on the town and the plains. The first elements of the Army of the Potomac crossed on December 11, 1862. The bulk of Burnside's men crossed the next day.

December 13 saw Union attacks on Lee's right flank, the segment under

Jackson's command, on a plain south of Fredericksburg. The main Union force moved against the Confederate left, under James Longstreet, solidly positioned on and in front of Marye's Heights, just west of town. Burnside called for a seemingly simple frontal assault—but this meant charging up a hill, against the heights and a stone wall just before it. Union troops did not even reach the wall before they were forced back by heavy fire. Burnside was talked out of renewing the attack the next day and Lee persuaded Jackson not to counterattack. On December 15, the Federals withdrew back across the river.

Just over a month later, on January 25, 1863, Burnside resigned as commander of the Army of the Potomac. That same day, Joseph Hooker was appointed as his replacement. Because of the miserable winter weather, Hooker had three months in which to reorganize his army. During this time Hooker grew tired of having his plans speculated upon, and perhaps given away, in northern newspapers. He decided one way to make reporters think twice about revealing Union plans in the papers was to require them to sign their pieces. Joseph Hooker thus created the modern newspaper byline.

By the time the spring campaigning season arrived, Hooker had a far better army than the one he had inherited from Burnside. He now had to use that tool to subdue the South. Jackson would play the primary role in Confederate attempts to ensure that Hooker failed.

Chancellorsville

Ten years after the battle of Chancellorsville, a writer described the area of the battle: "It is impossible to conceive a field worse adapted to the movements of a grand army. . . . The whole face of the country is thickly wooded, with only an occasional opening, and intersected by a few narrow wood-roads. . . . It was a region of gloom and the shadow of death."

Joseph Hooker had an army more than twice the size of Lee's. Lee had sent James Longstreet, with two divisions, to southern Virginia to obtain supplies. When word came that Hooker's troops were on the move, Longstreet was notified to return, but he could not make it back before Hooker attacked.

Hooker's attack started off well. His plans for the May 1863 operations were good, and he was confident, de-

"A Skirmish in the Wilderness," an 1864 painting by Winslow Homer, shows some of the dense vegetation and challenging terrain that the soldiers encountered at Chancellorsville. *(New Britain Museum of American Art)*

claring: "My plans are perfect, and when I start to carry them out, may God have mercy on General Lee, for I will have none." Part of Hooker's army, under John Sedgwick, was sent to create a diversion at Fredericksburg. The bulk of the army would then swing around Lee's left flank through the heavy forest called the Wilderness, lure Lee out of his fortifications near Fredericksburg, and destroy him in open battle. One Confederate officer later wrote, "On the whole I think this plan was decidedly the best strategy conceived in any of the campaigns ever set on foot against us." But even the best plans have to be properly executed.

Hooker's plan required careful coordination and communication among the various elements he commanded. Despite the use of the telegraph, communication was frequently problematic during the Civil War. In Robert E. Lee, Hooker faced an opponent likely to take advantage of any mistakes.

Until Hooker actually began to move his army, the Army of Northern Virginia, too, had the chance to rest. Jackson had two particularly appreciated visitors during this time. General Jackson was always reluctant to grant leaves to his men. The work of defending the Confederacy, which the religious Jackson also considered the work of God, was a full-time job. Jackson never took leave, and so rarely granted it to others. But he did allow soldiers' wives to visit. This included his own wife, Anna, who arrived on April 20, 1863, with their baby daughter, Julia. She had been born the previous November, and Jackson had not yet met her. Staff members say they never saw him happier than when his wife and daughter were visiting.

Hooker's Union forces began to move on Monday, April 27, 1863. April 27 and 28 saw the main force concentrating and moving northwest along the Rappahannock River. Another force, under John Sedgwick, made preparations for crossing this river just south of Fredericksburg. Several of Sedgwick's subordinate generals had suggested a real attack in this area. Speaking for Hooker, Chief of Staff Dan Butterfield, who was in charge of all army support and administrative services, wrote to Sedgwick: "Telegraph us freely early in the morning. Keep a good look at the size and number of campfires. It is very important to know whether or not the enemy are being held in your front. The moment news arrives with regard to the progress made to-day by the right wing, plans for to-morrow will issue. The maneuvers now in progress the general hopes will compel the enemy to fight him on his own ground. He has no desire to make the general engagement where you are."

The next day, Sedgwick was given orders authorizing him to attack if he noticed any Confederate weakness on his front. The Union diversion did not work. Lee never considered Sedgwick's advance to be Hooker's main effort. Later on April 29, Confederate cavalry detected Federal troops crossing into the Wilderness and sent word to Lee. This shifted Lee's attention back to the Wilderness and confirmed Lee's expectations of Union flanking efforts. Lee sent Richard Anderson's division, under Lee's direct command in the absence of Longstreet, to intercept the Union forces at the river crossing. After being informed of the close proximity of stronger Union forces, Lee ordered Anderson to pull back. In the hours before midnight, Anderson took a position not far from a house belonging to the family that gave its name to the area: the Chancellor family. That afternoon, Jackson's wife and daughter left camp for the relative safety of Richmond.

After sunrise, Anderson was able to get a better look at his division's position. The division was covering the roads they had been ordered to cover, but the thick woods around the roads made for poor visibility. Anderson's men might not be able to see flanking forces. Acting on his initiative, under Lee's discretionary orders, Anderson withdrew three miles to the east, to a position in the open, and began to entrench.

That afternoon, Lee realized what Hooker was planning. In an attempt to make the most of his comparatively meager forces, Lee risked the classic error of splitting his army with an enemy nearby. His move is still considered one of the most daring in military history: outnumbered two to one, he chose to divide his forces and attack on two fronts. He began to move Jackson's Second Corps divisions to intercept Hooker. General Jubal Early was left with his own division and some additional units to hold Fredericksburg against Sedgwick's forces on that front. Retreat was never considered an option. When Jackson heard that there were rumors of retreat within the army, he replied firmly, "We shall not fall back! We shall attack them!"

About noon, the Union Fifth Corps, under George Meade, began to arrive near Chancellorsville, Hooker's planned concentration point. A few hours later, talking with General Henry Slocum, commander of the Twelfth Corps, Meade expressed pleasure at how well the advance had gone. He proposed to Slocum that they continue the march and get out of the Wilderness as soon as possible. Meade was clearly disappointed when Slocum informed him that Hooker had ordered them to stay where they were, to await the arrival of the Second and

Third Corps. Meade even had to recall one of his units that had already pushed ahead and spotted entrenched Confederates.

Hooker's last major action that evening was to issue a statement to his army, summarizing progress so far: "It is with heartfelt satisfaction the commanding general announces to the army that the operations of the last three days have determined that our enemy must either ingloriously fly, or come out from behind his defenses and give us battle on our own ground."

Early in the morning of May 1, 1863, a usually reli-

During the Civil War, hot air balloons became common vessels for scouting. It was even possible to send a telegram from a balloon to the ground. Before Hooker eventually disbanded the Balloon Corps in 1863, soldiers had also begun to shoot upon the enemy from balloons. *(Library of Congress)*

able Union scout who observed Confederate movement from a hot air balloon, reported that Jackson's corps was still in the Fredericksburg area, facing Sedgwick. But the scout was wrong: Jackson had moved out with his troops. Hooker ordered an advance that morning into Chancellorsville. One division advanced east along the Orange Turnpike. Other units advanced along the Orange Plank Road to the south and the River Road to the north. At about this same time, Jackson ordered his men to advance west on the two southern roads.

George Meade's Fifth Corps met virtually no resistance on the River Road. The lead elements on the Orange Turnpike made contact with the Confederates, and fighting started about 11:30 AM. The situation on the parallel Orange Plank Road was more unusual. The Confederates on this road actually advanced past the Union forces on the Turnpike. In the thick woods, neither side was aware of the other's presence.

The Wilderness was a particularly bad place to fight a battle. The woods were thick, tangled, and deep. The smoke from weapons would have limited a soldier's range of vision even more. Because of the way battle was conducted in the late nineteenth century, commanders did not have direct control over their men, which made the battle of Chancellorsville more a series of small engagements than a major battle. Enemy bullets would come terrifyingly out of the mist, and the soldiers would have to shoot back into the mist at unseen targets. Clearings would not have come as a relief because they

The Chancellor house, Hooker's headquarters for the Union army. *(Library of Congress)*

only served to make the soldier an easier target.

The battle flowed back and forth for several hours. Union troops were pushed back on the Orange Turnpike by Confederate reinforcements, but the outcome of the battle as a whole was still an unanswered question. Hooker, however, ordered his men to withdraw to their positions of the previous evening. His corps commanders were surprised, believing that Hooker was giving up a fight that could be won. George Meade is reported to have asked in exasperation, "If he can't hold the top of the hill, how does he expect to hold the bottom?"

By May 1, Hooker was back at Chancellor house. Though he had superior numbers, by this point in the war Lee and Jackson had a tremendous psychological effect on both Confederate and Union troops. Their mere presence was enough to convince the Union forces that the Confederates had more men, more strength, and more of a chance for victory than they actually did. Hooker was losing his confidence that, as he had not long ago asserted, his own plans were perfect. More days of battle would follow and Hooker would have to make more decisions, but he had already made one very dangerous error. He had let the initiative pass to Lee and Jackson.

That evening, Lee and Jackson met to discuss how to take advantage of Hooker's withdrawal. Though the Union army had backed down, the Confederate commanders knew that only one of Hooker's three columns had been heavily pressed. The Union troops were still strong.

While Lee and Jackson were discussing attack options, including a flank attack, cavalry leader Jeb Stuart arrived to report that the far right flank of the Union line, Oliver Otis Howard's Eleventh Corps, was "in the air." It was then that Lee and Jackson made what became their famous decision to go after the Union right. Jackson would take his entire thirty-thousand-man corps for the assault, leaving Lee with only twenty thousand men to hold off Hooker's seventy-five thousand men nearby. They were taking a great chance.

Jackson met briefly with Lee early the next morning, May 2, 1863. No record exists of their discussion, but afterwards Jackson rode off and the march got underway. Jackson's route was not entirely hidden from his enemy, but this actually proved to be an advantage. Senior Union commanders, who were not taking active

Opposite: Jackson and Lee's last meeting, on the morning of May 2, 1863. *(Museum of the Confederacy, Richmond)*

measures to determine enemy intentions, thought the Confederates were withdrawing. This fit with Hooker's assertion that Lee would have to fight or flee. Sometime that day, though, Hooker finally guessed what Jackson might be up to. He sent word to the commander of his right flank to be ready. Apparently the message either never reached the commander or was ignored.

The march, though less than ten miles, was a difficult one for Jackson's men. They had been instructed to avoid talking, only whispering if they absolutely had to. Some of the men realized what Jackson was attempting, and knew that if he pulled it off it would be a major Southern victory. Anticipation in their ranks grew.

At about 2 PM, Jackson, at the head of his column, reached the Orange Plank Road. Brigadier General Fitz Lee, Lee's nephew, a Confederate cavalry commander, joined him. Lee suggested that Jackson ride with him to a point where they could get a clear view of the Union right flank. From there, Jackson saw that he needed to move his army another mile and a half before attacking.

By 5 PM, all was ready. Jackson looked at a group of officers around him, and saw that seventeen of them had been students or professors at VMI. "The Institute will be heard from today," he remarked. The attack began at 5:15, when Jackson asked former VMI Professor Robert Rodes, "Are you ready, General Rodes?" "Yes, sir," Rodes replied. "You can go forward, then," Jackson said calmly.

The first sign the Union forces had of the Confederate

The battle of Chancellorsville. *(Library of Congress)*

attack was thousands of soldiers crashing out of the woods, crumbling most of the Union right. Encroaching darkness eventually halted the Confederates. Still, the rest of the Union troops had been alerted by the noise and given time to prepare. The Southern troops then became disorganized by their own success. They would have to be straightened out before further advances would be feasible.

Jackson planned a night attack, a rarity at the time. His goal was to cut off Hooker's primary route of retreat to safety across the Rappahannock River. Jackson decided to go take a personal look over the ground. He first stopped at the headquarters of Jim Lane, commander of a brigade from North Carolina. Lane's brigade was in advance of the rest of Jackson's force, and in a potentially vulnerable position. They had stopped their advance due to heavy Union artillery fire in front of them. Lane moved his largest regiment, the Thirty-seventh North Carolina, into a skirmish line to guard the brigade and give early warning of an attack. He also told his men to pay particular attention to a thick grove of oak trees across the road from their position.

After a brief conversation with A. P. Hill, Jackson's senior division commander, Jackson rode forward with a few of his aides. They were on their way to the river where they would examine the territory. They rode through the lines of the Eighteenth North Carolina, which had been told about the scouting mission. A. P. Hill and some of his aides followed Jackson's party at a distance. Jackson rode to within two hundred yards of the Federal lines, close enough to hear commands being given. He and his aides then turned and rode slowly back to their own lines. As they did, several shots rang out, and then a volley. One of Jackson's aides, Jim Morrison, who was also Jackson's brother-in-law, ran towards the line of the Eighteenth North Carolina and told them to stop shooting, that they were shooting their own men. In confusion, the officer in command of that regiment, Major John D. Barry, responded, "Who gave that order? It's a lie! Pour it to them, boys!"

Three bullets hit Jackson at the same time. One splintered the bones in his upper left arm before passing through completely. The second bullet went through his lower left arm. The third entered the palm of his right hand, broke two fingers, and remained lodged there. His beloved horse, Little Sorrel, bolted at the noise, and ran Jackson right into a low-hanging branch that cut up his face and nearly knocked him off his mount. Two of Jackson's aides helped bring his horse under control. The general was in intense pain.

Both his party and Hill's had been hit. Of the nineteen men, ten were casualties of friendly fire (a term coined in the twentieth century to describe accidentally firing upon your own side). Hill and some of Jackson's aides quickly cut the left sleeve of his coat to determine the seriousness of his wounds. As they were working, two Union soldiers stepped out of the woods less than five yards from Jackson. Hill shouted for his men to grab the Union soldiers. It was clear the wounded Jackson would have to be moved from between the lines.

A litter was found and several men began to carry Jackson to a place of safety where he could receive treatment from his medical director, Dr. Hunter McGuire. Before they got very far, Union troops began shelling. A piece of shell struck and knocked down one of the litter bearers. Jackson was dropped off the litter, which had been carried at shoulder level, and fell five feet to the ground. He landed on his wounded left shoulder with a loud groan. Hill was wounded in the same shelling.

A few hours later, Jackson's party finally reached safety behind Confederate lines. Dr. Hunter McGuire caught up with them there and did what he could before riding with Jackson to a field hospital farther back from the lines. After midnight on May 3, McGuire and several other surgeons put Jackson to sleep with chloroform and then amputated his left arm. This was the most common practice for treating arm and leg wounds—antibiotics had not yet been developed, and without them any wound could become infected and eventually kill the patient. The large, soft bullet of the 1860s made a wound that would be hard to treat even with today's medicine.

Later that day, Jackson had recovered enough to speak. He complained to McGuire about a pain on his left side. McGuire could not determine its source, but the pain soon abated. Jackson learned that, since Hill was wounded and Rodes was too junior, command had been given to Jeb Stuart. When Stuart asked for instructions, Jackson just told him to do what he thought best.

What Stuart thought best was to press the Union troops heavily. The May 3 fighting was some of the toughest and bloodiest in the Civil War. Hooker's main force was pushed back, but to a strong position anchored on the Rappahannock River. Sedgwick's forces in Fredericksburg, after advancing to and then being pushed back from Salem Church, formed a similar salient, or line of defense, a few miles to the east. Both forces were safely withdrawn a couple of nights later, perhaps anticipating Lee's planned attack.

Still later on May 3, a message arrived from Lee saying that Jackson should be moved even farther back from the lines. Lee had earlier expressed his deep regret

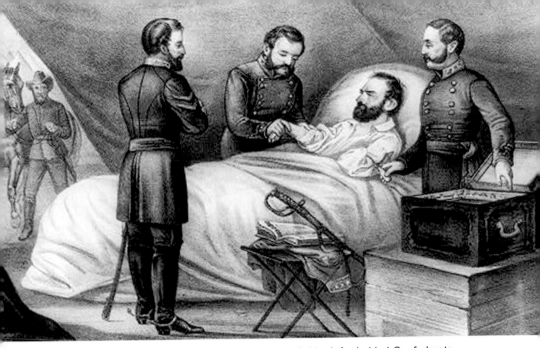

A badly wounded Stonewall Jackson in a hospital bed, far behind Confederate lines at Chancellorsville. *(Library of Congress)*

at Jackson being wounded, and now he wanted his prized general moved to safety. McGuire approved, so Jackson endured another wagon ride, this time to Guinea Station, about fifteen miles due south of Fredericksburg. Arriving the evening of May 4, after a fourteen-hour trip, Jackson was given a bed where he could rest. He bore the trip well, but his left side was hurting again and he felt nauseated.

The next day Jackson received sympathy and encouragement from Lee, who had asked the messenger to tell Jackson: "He has lost his left arm but I my right arm." Lee had gone on, "Tell him to get well and come back to me as soon as he can."

Things seemed to be going well for Jackson until around one in the morning on May 7. He awoke with a great pain in his side, feverish and nauseated. Always a believer in water cures, Jackson asked for a wet towel to bathe his side. By dawn, Jackson was in even more pain and having trouble breathing. McGuire was summoned. Examining Jackson, he concluded that Jackson had contracted pneumonia. McGuire did what he could, but with the medical knowledge of the time, pneumonia was a death sentence.

Jackson's wife was summoned from Richmond, and she arrived around noon the same day. Jackson was very pleased to see her. But, for the next few days, his steadily worsening condition, combined with the narcotics he was given as painkillers, sent him in and out of consciousness and delirium. Mentally, he found himself back on the battlefield, and he could be heard giving orders to aides present only in his mind. By May 10, Dr. McGuire realized that Jackson could not last the day. He informed Anna, and she gave Jackson the news.

At 3:15 that afternoon, Jackson's mind took him far

This fanciful drawing shows an imagined memorial to Stonewall Jackson at his childhood home in West Virginia. *(Library of Congress)*

This photograph of Jackson, called the "Chancellorsville Photograph," was taken only two weeks before he was mortally wounded. *(VMI Archives, Lexington)*

from the battlefield to Jackson's Mill, his boyhood home. Stonewall Jackson uttered his last words, "Let us cross over the river, and rest under the shade of the trees," then died.

A year later, Abraham Lincoln was reelected president of the United States. His second inaugural address,

Lee's surrender to Grant at the Appomattox Court House in Virginia on April 9, 1865. *(Appomattox Court House National Historic Park)*

offered in March of 1865, closed with these famous lines: "With malice toward none, with charity for all, with firmness in the right as God gives us to see the right, let us strive on to finish the work we are in, to bind up the nation's wounds, to care for him who shall have borne the battle and for his widow and his orphan, to do all which may achieve and cherish a just and lasting peace among ourselves and with all nations."

One month later, on April 9, 1865, the Civil War officially ended when the Confederate general Robert

E. Lee surrendered to Union general Ulysses S. Grant at Appomattox. Five days later, on April 14, President Lincoln was assassinated while attending a performance at Ford's Theater. Had he lived, he doubtless would have been disappointed that Reconstruction of the South and the reunification of the United States was neither quickly nor easily accomplished. The legacy of the Civil War, which killed over 600,000 Americans, was not one of peace and reconciliation but of lasting resentment, bitterness, and a long, slow process of recovery.

During the difficult years after the war's end, Stonewall Jackson came to symbolize for many people the bravery and determination of the Civil War soldiers. Reconstruction and its aftermath were particularly hard on the South, and some people there seized upon Jackson as a reminder of the potential of courage, perseverance, and self-sacrifice. His iconic status, though earned over the course of his military career, was perhaps enhanced by his untimely death. Monuments to his name and his courage still stand, and his name, used even today by the Stonewall Brigade of the Virginia National Guard, continues to evoke the image of a purposeful, resolute man.

Timeline

1824   Born on January 21 in Clarksburg, Virginia (now West Virginia).

1826   Jackson's father and older sister die within a week of each other; Jackson's younger sister, Laura, is born one day after his father dies.

1830   Mother Julia remarries.

1831   Jackson and sister sent to live with uncle; older brother, Warren, goes to live with mother's family; Laura sent to different relatives; Julia Jackson dies on December 4 at age thirty-three.

1841   Warren Jackson, age twenty, dies of tuberculosis.

1842   Jackson enters West Point.

1846   Graduates West Point, seventeenth of fifty-nine graduates.

1846-   Serves in Mexican War.
1848

1848-   Peacetime military service in New York and Florida.
1851

1851-   Teaches at Virginia Military Institute.
1861

1853   Marries Elinor Junkin on August 4.

1854   Elinor dies in childbirth on October 22; child is stillborn.

1857   Jackson marries Mary Anna Morrison on July 16.

1859   Helps lead VMI contingent providing security at John Brown's execution on December 2.

1861   Takes command of Virginia state units at Harpers Ferry; promoted to brigadier general in July; wins nickname "Stonewall" at the first battle of Bull Run (July); promoted to major general and placed in command of Shenandoah Valley (October).

May-June 1862	Jackson's Shenandoah Valley campaign.
June 1862	Seven Days campaign.
August 1862	Battle of Cedar Mountain.
August 28-30, 1862	Battles of Groveton and second Bull Run.
September 1, 1862	Battle of Chantilly.
September 15, 1862	Jackson captures large Federal garrison at Harpers Ferry.
September 17, 1862	Battle of Antietam.
November, 1862	Daughter Julia born.
December 13, 1862	Battle of Fredericksburg.
May 1, 1863	Start of battle of Chancellorsville.
May 2, 1863	Jackson's flank march routs right flank of Federal army; Jackson wounded by his own men in dark.
May 5, 1863	Battle of Chancellorsville ends with Union withdrawal.
May 10, 1863	Jackson dies.
July 1-3, 1863	Battle of Gettysburg.
April 8, 1865	Army of Northern Virginia surrenders at Appomattox Court House, Virginia.

Sources

CHAPTER ONE: Forging His Path

p. 14, "Uncle was like a father . . ." Thomas Jackson Arnold, *Early Life and Letters of General Thomas J. Jackson* (New York: Fleming H. Revell, 1916), 162.

p. 14, "none to give the mandates . . ." Holmes Moss Alexander, *The Hidden Years* (Richwood: West Virginia Press Club, 1981), 24.

p. 17, "That fellow looks . . ." Dabney H. Maury, *Recollection of a Virginian in the Mexican, Indian, and Civil Wars* (New York: Charles Scribner's Sons, 1894), 22-23.

p. 18, "go through or die," James I. Robertson, Jr., *Stonewall Jackson: The Man, the Soldier, the Legend* (New York: Simon and Schuster MacMillan, 1997), 35.

p. 19, "You may be . . ." Byron Farwell, *Stonewall: A Biography of General Thomas J. Jackson* (New York: W. W. Norton & Company, 1992), 27.

p. 21, "I am still living . . ." Robertson, *Stonewall Jackson*, 85.

CHAPTER TWO: First Taste of Combat

p. 23, "rumor appears to indicate . . ." Robertson, *Stonewall Jackson*, 38.

p. 29, "I really envy you men . . ." Ibid., 52.

p. 30, "Allowing the enemy to retire . . ." Ibid., 55.

p. 31, "fill[ed] me with . . ." Ibid., 57.

p. 32, "I presume you think . . ." Farwell, *Stonewall*, 45.

p. 36, "Oh, never . . ." Robert Lewis Dabney, *Life and Campaigns of Lieut.-Gen. Thomas J. Jackson (Stonewall*

Jackson) (New York: Blelock, 1866), 52.

p. 39, "I don't know if I will shake hands . . ." Robertson, *Stonewall Jackson,* 70.

CHAPTER THREE: Peacetime Soldier and Teacher

p. 44, "I like scouting very much . . ." Farwell, *Stonewall,* 77.

p. 49, "hour angle of the sun . . . letter of his instructions," Virginia Military Institute, "James A. Walker Court Martial," http://www.vmi.edu/archives/Jackson/tjjcourt.html.

p. 53, "My little pet, your husband . . ." Robertson, *Stonewall Jackson,* 194.

p. 53, "It has been said that General Jackson . . ." Mary Anna Jackson, *Memoirs of Stonewall Jackson, by his Widow* (Louisville, Kentucky: The Prentice Press, 1895), 141-143.

p. 54, "We are looking to . . ." David Flavel Jamison, letter, *Charleston Daily Courier,* November 3, 1859.

p. 55, "a firebell in the night . . . filled me with terror," Paul Leicester Ford, ed., *Writings of Thomas Jefferson,* Volume X (New York: Putnam's, 1892-1899), 157-158.

p. 56, "fault line," Samuel Huntington, "The Clash of Civilizations," *Foreign Affairs* 72, no. 3 (Summer 1993): 22.

p. 56, "geographic line . . ." Ford, *Writings of Thomas Jefferson,* 158.

p. 58, "The South never made . . ." *Louisville Democrat,* December 30, 1857.

CHAPTER FOUR: Stonewall

p. 59, "At this time . . ." Anna Jackson, *Memoirs,* 139.

p. 60, "Although the enterprise . . ." Robertson, *Stonewall Jackson,* 175.

p. 61, "There are about 1,000 troops . . ." Burke Davis, *They Called Him Stonewall* (New York: Fairfax Press, 1954), 6.

p. 62, "John Brown was . . ." Robertson, *Stonewall Jackson,* 199.

p. 62, "heard and saw . . ." Robertson, *Stonewall Jackson,* 203.

p. 63, "The last party . . ." *Charleston Mercury,* May 3, 1860.

p. 64, "I am in favor . . ." Arnold, *Early Life,* 293.

p. 65, "after we have done . . ." Robertson, *Stonewall Jackson,* 207.

p. 66, "Military men make short . . ." James Harvey Wood, *The War: "Stonewall" Jackson, His Campaigns and Battles, the Regiment as I Saw Them* (Gaithersburg, Maryland: Butternut Press, 1984), 11.

p. 69, "When a cloud comes . . ." Robertson, *Stonewall Jackson,* 691.

p. 72, "General Jackson . . . seen it before," Ibid., 264.

p. 73, "There were carriages . . ." Richard Wheeler, *A Rising Thunder* (New York: HarperPerennial, 1994), 352.

p. 75, "a battle always had the effect . . ." Robertson, *Stonewall Jackson,*195.

p. 76, "General, they are . . . Follow me!" Ibid., 264.

p. 80, "You are the *First Brigade! . . ."* John Esten Cooke, *Stonewall Jackson: A Military Biography* (New York: G.W. Dillingham [n.d.]), 76.

CHAPTER FIVE: Stonewall in the Valley

p. 81, "Its eastern wall . . ." George Edward Pond, *The Shenandoah Valley in 1864* (New York: Charles Scribner's Sons, 1905), 1-2.

p. 85, "these mounds were burst . . ." Robertson, *Stonewall Jackson,* 307.

p. 85, "I have halted to let the men . . . this brigade," G. F. R. Henderson, *Stonewall Jackson and the American Civil War* (London and New York: Longmans, Green and Co., 1898), 144.

p. 87, "With such interference . . ." Robertson, *Stonewall Jackson,* 317.

p. 93, "I want you to make me a map of the Valley . . ." Jedediah Hotchkiss, *Make Me a Map of the Valley* (Dallas: Southern Methodist University Press, 1973), 10.

p. 98, "I am of the opinion . . ." *War of the Rebellion: Official Records of the Union and Confederate Armies* (Washington, D.C.: Government Printing Office, 1880-1900, Series I, Volume XII, Part 3), 898.

p. 98, "Suspend the execution of . . ." Ibid.

p. 98, "The whole question is whether . . ." Robert G. Tanner, *Stonewall in the Valley* (New York: Doubleday and Company, 1976), 201.

CHAPTER SIX: Return to Bull Run

p. 105, "Do you know we are losing valuable time . . ." *Philadelphia Weekly Times,* April 20, 1878.

p. 111, "by advising your division commanders . . ." Robert Edward Lee, *The Wartime Papers of R.E. Lee* (Boston: Little, Brown, 1961), 239.

p. 112, "Banks is in our front . . ." Hunter George McGuire and George L. Christian, *The Confederate Cause and Conduct in the War Between the States* (Richmond: L. H. Jenkins, 1907), 527.

p. 112, "fell with great vigor . . ." *Official Records,* Series I, Volume XII, Part 2, 183.

p. 113, "I thought the heavens . . ." Robertson, *Stonewall Jackson,* 534.

p. 113, "Jackson usually is an indifferent . . ." Ibid., 532.

p. 117, "my ammunition is . . ." Farwell, *Stonewall,* 496.

p. 118, "Tell him that . . ." Ibid.

p. 118, "I'll expect you to beat them . . ." Ibid.

p. 118, "We slaughtered them . . ." Ibid.

p. 118, "Tell him I knew . . ." *Philadelphia Weekly Times,* April 20, 1878.

p. 119, "Late in the evening . . ." *Official Records,* Series I, Volume XIX, Part 2, 590.

CHAPTER SEVEN: Invading the North

p. 121, "The present seems to be the most . . ." *Official Records,* Series I, Volume XII, Part 2, 647.

p. 124, "Such criticisms were obvious . . ." William Allan, *The Army of Northern Virginia in 1862* (Dayton, Ohio: Morningside House, 1984), 200.

p. 126, "There are but few commanders . . ." Robert K. Krick, "Maxcy Gregg: Political Extremist and Confederate General," *Civil War History,* Volume 19 (1975), 307-308.

p. 127, "Enemy reported in . . ." Paul R. Teetor, *A Matter of Hours* (Rutherford, New Jersey: Fairleigh Dickinson University Press, 1982), 97.

p. 129, "Now I know what to do . . ." Stephen W. Sears, *George B. McClellan: The Young Napoleon* (New York: Ticknor & Fields, 1988), 280.

p. 130, "Through God's blessing . . ." Robertson, *Stonewall Jackson,* 605.

p. 131, "The design was . . ." *Official Records,* Series I, Volume XIX, part 1, 30.

p. 133, "I think they . . ." Robertson, *Stonewall Jackson,* 617.

p. 136, "We were so badly . . ." Ronald H. Bailey and the editors of Time-Life Books, *The Battle of Antietam* (Alexandria, Virginia: Time-Life Books, 1984), 139.

p. 139, "The army in Virginia . . ." Peter W. Alexander, *Savannah Republican,* reprinted in *Macon Journal & Messenger,* October 8, 1862.

CHAPTER EIGHT: Chancellorsville

p. 142, "It is impossible . . ." Theodore Irving, *More Than Conqueror: Memorials of J. Howard Kitching* (New York:

Hurd and Houghton [n.d.]), 124.

p. 143, "My plans are perfect . . ." Stephen W. Sears, *Chancellorsville* (Boston: Houghton Mifflin Company, 1996), 120.

p. 143, "On the whole . . ." Edward Porter Alexander, *Fighting for the Confederacy,* ed. Gary W. Gallagher (Chapel Hill and London: The University of North Carolina Press, 1989), 195.

p. 144, "Telegraph us freely . . ." *Official Records,* Series I, Volume XXV, part 2, 292.

p. 146, "We shall not fall back . . ." Farwell, *Stonewall,* 493.

p. 147, "It is with heartfelt satisfaction . . ." *Official Records,* Series I, Volume XXIII, part 1, 171.

p. 149, "If he can't hold the top of the hill . . ." John Bigelow, Jr., *The Campaign of Chancellorsville* (New Haven: Yale University Press, 1910), 154.

p. 152, "The Institute will be heard from . . ." Robertson, *Stonewall Jackson,* 721.

p. 152, "Are you ready, General Rodes? . . ." Farwell, *Stonewall,* 503.

p. 154, "Who gave that order? . . ." Robertson, *Stonewall Jackson,* 728.

p. 157, "He has lost his . . ." Ibid., 746.

p. 159, "Let us cross over the river . . ." Ibid., 753.

Bibliography

Alexander, Bevin. *Lost Victories: The Military Genius of Stonewall Jackson.* New York: Holt, 1992.

Alexander, Edward Porter. *Fighting for the Confederacy: The Personal Recollections of General Edward Porter Alexander.* Edited by Gary W. Gallagher. Chapel Hill and London: University of North Carolina Press, 1989.

Alexander, Holmes Moss. *The Hidden Years.* Richwood: West Virginia Press Club, 1981.

Allan, William. *The Army of Northern Virginia in 1862.* Dayton, Ohio: Morningside House, 1984.

Arnold, Thomas Jackson. *Early Life and Letters of General Thomas J. Jackson, "Stonewall" Jackson, by his nephew, Thomas Jackson Arnold.* New York, Chicago: Fleming H. Revell Company, 1916.

Bailey, Ronald H. and the editors of Time-Life Books. *The Battle of Antietam.* Alexandria, Virginia: Time-Life Books, 1984.

Bigelow, John Jr. *The Campaign of Chancellorsville.* New Haven: Yale University Press, 1910.

Canning, Steven A. *Crisis of Fear.* New York: Simon and Schuster, 1970.

Cooke, John Esten. *Stonewall Jackson: A Military Biography.* New York: G.W. Dillingham [n.d.].

Dabney, Robert Lewis. *Life and Campaigns of Lieut-Gen. Thomas J. Jackson (Stonewall Jackson).* New York: Blelock, 1866.

Davis, Burke. *They Called Him Stonewall: A Life of Lt. General T. J. Jackson, C.S.A.* New York: Fairfax Press, 1954.

Eisenhower, John S. D. *So Far From God: The U.S. War with Mexico, 1846-1848.* New York: Random House, 1989.

Farwell, Byron. *Stonewall: A Biography of General Thomas J. Jackson.* New York: W. W. Norton & Company, 1992.

Ford, Paul Leicester, ed. *Writings of Thomas Jefferson,* Volume X. New York: Putnam's, 1882-1899.

Happel, Ralph. *Jackson.* Richmond, Virginia: Eastern National Park and Monument Association, 1971.

Henderson, G. F. R. *Stonewall Jackson and the American Civil War.* London and New York: Longmans, Green and Co., 1898.

Hotchkiss, Jedediah. *Make Me a Map of the Valley.* Dallas: Southern Methodist University Press, 1973.

Huntington, Samuel. "The Clash of Civilizations." *Foreign Affairs,* Vol. 72, no. 3 (Summer 1993), 22-50.

Irving, Theodore. *More Than Conqueror: Memorials of J. Howard Kitching.* New York: Hurd and Houghton, 1872.

Jackson, Mary Anna. *Memoirs of Stonewall Jackson, by his Widow.* Louisville, Kentucky: The Prentice Press, 1895.

Keegan, John. *Intelligence in War.* New York: Alfred A. Knopf, 2003.

Krick, Robert K. "Maxcy Gregg: Political Extremist and Confederate General." *Civil War History.* Volume 19 (1975), 307-308.

Lee, Robert Edward. *The Wartime Papers of R. E. Lee.* Boston: Little, Brown, 1961.

Maury, Dabney H. *Recollections of a Virginian in the Mexican, Indian and Civil Wars.* New York: Charles Scribner's Sons, 1894.

McGuire, Hunter George and George L. Christian. *The Confederate Cause and Conduct in the War Between the States.*

Richmond: L. H. Jenkins, 1907.

Pond, George Edward. *The Shenandoah Valley in 1864.* New York: Charles Scribner's Sons, 1885.

Robertson, James I., Jr. *Stonewall Jackson.* New York: MacMillan, 1997.

Sears, Stephen W. *Chancellorsville.* Boston: Houghton Mifflin Company, 1996.

————. *George B. McClellan: The Young Napoleon.* New York: Ticknor & Fields, 1988.

Simpson, Brooks D. *America's Civil War.* Wheeling, Illinois: Harlan Davidson, 1996.

Stackpole, Edward J. *From Cedar Mountain to Antietam.* Harrisburg, Pennsylvania: The Stackpole Company, 1959.

Tanner, Robert G. *Stonewall in the Valley.* New York: Doubleday and Company, Inc., 1976.

Teetor, Paul. *A Matter of Hours.* Rutherford, New Jersey: Fairleigh Dickinson University, 1982.

United States War Department. *War of the Rebellion: Official Records of the Union and Confederate Armies.* Washington, D.C.: Government Printing Office, 1880-1900.

Vandiver, Frank E. *Mighty Stonewall.* New York: McGraw-Hill, 1957.

Virginia Military Institute Archives. Web site: www.new.vmi.edu/archives/Jackson

Wheeler, Richard. *A Rising Thunder.* New York: HarperPerennial, 1994.

Wood, James Harvey. *The War: "Stonewall" Jackson, His Campaigns and Battles, the Regiment as I Saw Them.* Gaithersburg, Maryland: Butternut Press, 1984.

Web sites

Stonewall Jackson Resources—VMI Archives
www.vmi.edu/archives/jackson/jackson.html
The section of the Virginia Military Institute's Web site
dedicated to Stonewall Jackson. It includes photographs,
Jackson's papers and letters, and a detailed biography.

National Park Service's Antietam Image Gallery
www.nps.gov/anti/gallery/htm
This site contains modern-day and historic photographs,
sketches, and paintings of the battlefield at Antietam.

Stonewall Jackson House
www.stonewalljackson.org/
The official Web site of Jackson's Lexington home, now a
museum owned by the Stonewall Jackson Foundation,
offers a brief biography and information about the museum.

The Mexican War and After
www.army.mil/cmh-pg/books/AMH/AMH-08.htm
The United States Army's official history of the Mexican
War.

Selected Civil War Photographs
http://memory.loc.gov/ammem/cwphtml/cwphome.html
The Library of Congress holds thousands of Civil War
photographs, many of which can be viewed at this site.

Index